I0065216

MASTERING
FLOW

IMPLEMENTATION GUIDEBOOK
for **GOLDRATT'S RULES OF FLOW
IN PROJECT ENVIRONMENTS**

MASTERING
FLOW

IMPLEMENTATION GUIDEBOOK
for **GOLDRATT'S RULES OF FLOW**
IN PROJECT ENVIRONMENTS

RAMI GOLDRATT & AJAI KAPOOR

North River Press

The North River Press Publishing Corporation

P.O. Box 567

Great Barrington, MA 01230

(800) 486-2665 or (413) 528-0034

www.northriverpress.com

For more information regarding the ideas presented in this book go to:

www.goldrattgroup.com

Copyright © 2025 Rami Goldratt and Ajai Kapoor.

ISBN: 978-088427-3059

All rights reserved, including those for text and data mining, AI training, and similar technologies. No part of this book may be reproduced or utilized in any form or by any means, electronic or mechanical, including photocopying, recording, or any information storage retrieval system, without permission in writing from the publisher.

ABOUT THE AUTHORS

Rami Goldratt serves as the CEO of Goldratt Group, founded by his father, Dr. Eliyahu Goldratt, with a mission to support managers in achieving breakthrough results using the Theory of Constraints (TOC). Rami has consulted for a wide array of industries worldwide and is considered one of the most influential leaders in the TOC body of knowledge, particularly in Sales and Marketing, where his work has become standard practice. Rami is passionate about explaining complex matters in a simple and easy-to-understand manner. He continues his father's legacy to drive innovation and excellence within the TOC framework.

Dr. Ajai Kapoor is a passionate practitioner of TOC, having dedicated the last 25 years to the field. Currently a Managing Partner at Goldratt Consulting North America, he has been an innovator in developing unique and simple solutions for some of the largest TOC consulting engagements. Ajai worked closely with Dr. Eliyahu Goldratt during the development of TOC applications for multi-project environments, and he has applied these methods across various industries. Today, Ajai is recognized as one of the world's leaders in this field. He is also the winner of the prestigious Fulkerson Prize, awarded by the Mathematical Programming Society and the American Mathematical Society.

CONTENTS

❞ In projects, like in production, the key is to understand the interconnection between logistics, human behavior, policies, and measurements. Any attempt to separate them will require mammoth efforts and result in nothing but sophisticated, impressive, yet useless methods. *❞*

Dr. Eliyahu Goldratt, *Project Management the TOC Way*

ACKNOWLEDGMENTS

First and foremost, we would like to acknowledge Dr. Eliyahu Goldratt, the creator of the Theory of Constraints, for his wisdom, knowledge, and mentorship, which have been a guiding light in our lives. This book builds on what we've learned from numerous TOC implementations, distilling his insights into practical methods, developed and refined by the experts at the Goldratt Group.

Specifically, we would like to thank our customers who have offered us opportunities to work with their teams to implement TOC solutions to improve flow. They displayed courage in implementing new ideas that ran counter to established conventional practices. We extend our heartfelt gratitude to all the experts at Goldratt, whose relentless efforts in developing and implementing TOC solutions have revolutionized project management across diverse industries and sectors.

We would like to especially thank Jaideep Srivastav, Sridhar Chandra, and Dr. Yishai Ashlag for the long association over which the knowledge and insights in this book were developed. Special thanks to Yuji Kishira for his insights on how the ideas described here contribute to bringing harmony back into organizations as highlighted in his book, *WA: Transformation Management by Harmony*. We extend our deepest gratitude to Dr. Efrat Goldratt-Ashlag for her invaluable contribution through her work, *Goldratt's Rules of Flow*, which vividly brings to life the realities of project environments and the possible transformation TOC can create. Efrat was very helpful in reviewing and supporting the creation of this implementation guidebook to make it accessible to people worldwide.

READY, SET, GO!

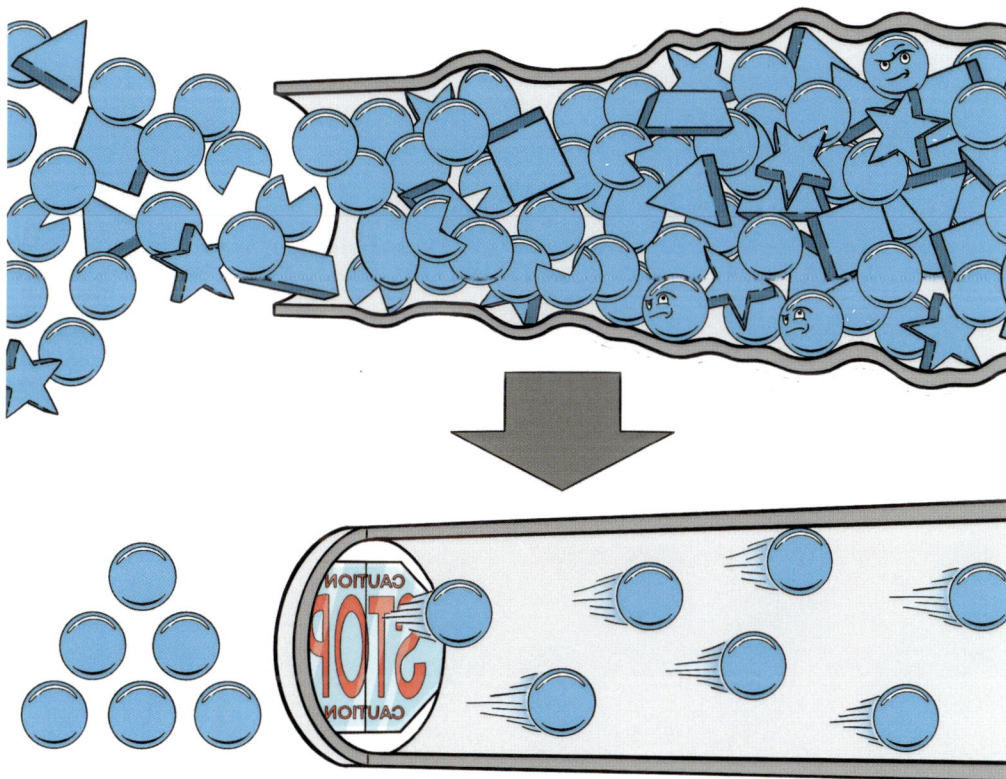

READY

This implementation guidebook for *Goldratt's Rules of Flow* shares decades of experience, in helping managers across industries to get more projects out the door faster.

- You will learn how we apply the Theory of Constraints (TOC) methodology to improve operations by addressing dominant obstacles to flow.

- You will understand how we boost the flow of operations in engineering, IT, construction, R&D, product development, administrative projects, government work, and many other project environments.

- You will learn how to identify the dominant obstacles to flow in your environment, the solutions you need to apply to remove these obstacles, and how to drive change to accelerate flow.

We are confident you will find much of what you read here highly relevant to your operations. If you are at the beginning of your business life, this guidebook will prepare you for what is to come. We hope that after reading this guidebook, you will no longer accept the status quo but will implement the necessary steps to achieve a leap in performance.

SET

As experienced managers, we are all aware that the work in project environments is usually non-standard and full of uncertainties. Companies that design or engineer products must meet the unique needs of each client. Service providers have to cater to the requirements of each customer which are often quite diverse. Organizations working on new and innovative products face unknowns by default. Maintenance and repair projects often deal with unexpected issues that only become clear after the work starts. IT projects solve specific business problems, which makes designing and building these systems a unique and unpredictable process.

Estimating how long tasks will take, how much they'll cost, or what resources are needed is essentially a forecast—and like any forecast it is often wrong. This uncertainty makes it hard to manage work effectively, leading to delays, overspending, or missed commitments.

On top of that, non-standard work relies heavily on experts to plan and execute tasks properly. But experts are hard to find because their knowledge comes from years of experience. This dependency causes delays, as work often waits for their input. When experts are stretched too thin and forced to multitask, their response time slows down, delaying projects even more and lowering productivity.

In addition to the non-standard nature of work, projects often entail a synchronization nightmare. Coordinating activities and resources to make progress on projects is very challenging. It is common to find work waiting for a resource to become available. Similarly, team members often cannot start an activity because some inputs such as information, materials, designs, authorization, and other resources that were supposed to be ready, are missing. Each task manager and resource manager operate with their own key performance indicators (KPIs) and local priorities, which can create conflicting goals. The variability in lead times, driven by the non-standard nature of the work, makes it nearly impossible to accurately schedule and coordinate the activities of everyone involved.

To make things worse, in order to remain competitive, we are under pressure to deliver more and more projects with the same (or sometimes less) resources and deliver them faster. Speeding up project delivery can be leveraged to create differentiation in the marketplace and to better deal with cash or labor constraints for healthy growth.

Flow is the pace at which work progresses and projects are completed. Improving the flow of project work should, therefore, be a prime objective for any organization. When we focus on improving project flow, we should keep in mind Dr. Eliyahu Goldratt's memorable saying: *Every improvement is a change, but certainly, not every change is an improvement.*[1] We should properly address three questions: What to change? What to change to? How to cause the change?

WHAT TO CHANGE?

As managers who have worked in the field for quite some time, we have all been investing a fair amount of effort attempting to improve performance. But, even if we manage to

---

[1] See Chapter 2 in Eliyahu M. Goldratt's (1999) *What is this thing called Theory of Constraints?* North River Press Publishing Corporation.

improve lead times, reliability, and productivity, it often feels like an uphill battle—just when we make progress, the work piles up again, and we end up back where we started. Sisyphus must have been a manager in a project-based environment.

Does this align with your environment? Go over the following challenges and mark to what extent you have experienced each one in your organization:

1	Long wait times for key resources	low	medium	high
2	Difficulty in meeting commitments	low	medium	high
3	Multitasking and delays across projects	low	medium	high
4	Difficulty in managing resources efficiently	low	medium	high
5	Constantly changing priorities	low	medium	high
6	Difficulty in scaling operations	low	medium	high
7	Loss of quality and high levels of rework	low	medium	high
8	Last minute surprises and delays	low	medium	high

If you have marked most of these challenges as "low", it suggests you have already mastered projects flow and you might find the solutions in this book unnecessary. If you experince similar challenges in your environement, it means we need to do something different. Very different.

According to Dr. Eliyahu Goldratt, to improve flow and complete more projects faster, we must challenge deeply rooted practices concerning the way we execute project work. One cannot expect substantial flow improvements by applying the same tactics used repeatedly before. As elaborated in the next chapters, we will continue to experience significant delays, rework, and stress as long as we:

● Attempt to achieve project headway and demonstrate progress by starting projects and tasks as early as possible and handing off work to the next phase prematurely.

● Attempt to gain project visibility and control by creating overly detailed project plans and imposing strict measurements related to on-time task completion.

This is what Goldratt's approach is all about. Such practices invariably result in bad multitasking, which greatly diminishes productivity. They cause frequent work stoppages due to missing work elements and information. They lead to reduced work dosages, causing tasks to loop back for further work, thereby delaying completion times. We experience horrendous desynchronization of resources and activities, which manifests as significant delays and rework at advanced stages of the project. Additionally, these practices overload our scarce experts, jeopardizing the ability to standardize work and scale the operation and to top it all, they waste the precious buffers needed to manage uncertainty effectively.

WHAT TO CHANGE TO?

To change the above practices and break vicious cycles in project work, we must start by restricting the WIP (Work In Process) level of projects and tasks in the system. Dr. Eliyahu Goldratt called it *establishing a practical mechanism that guides the operation when NOT to Produce (to prevent overproduction)*.[2] Overcoming the tendency to release and hand off work as early as possible will greatly improve flow. Once the WIP is restricted, we should continue to eliminate any major friction that slows down the flow. The mechanism to restrict open work and speed up flow is done by tackling prevailing obstacles to flow in your environment.

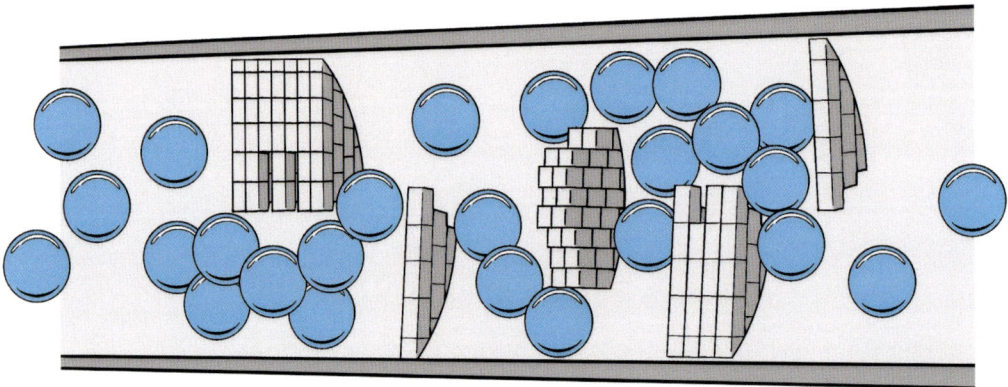

---

[2] See Dr. Eliyahu Goldratt's iconic article *Standing on the Shoulders of Giants*. This article can be found in Eliyahu, M. Goldratt's (2014) *The Goal: Process of Ongoing Improvement*. North River Press Corporation.

This implementation guidebook covers the most common obstacles to flow and the way to overcome them:

CHAPTER 2 | TRIAGE THE PROJECTS

When a surfeit of low-value projects disrupts the focus on and progress of high-value projects, delaying their completion and compromising the scope and quality of their outcomes.

CHAPTER 3 | REDUCE BAD MULTITASKING

When team members switch among too many projects and tasks without completing any.

CHAPTER 4 | SEGREGATE BIG AND SMALL TASKS

When the same team members handle a mix of low-load and high-load jobs, ending up compromising the delivery of all jobs.

CHAPTER 5 | ENSURE FULL-KIT

When too often, projects, or project phases, come to a halt or require rework because they were initiated without all the necessary requirements to adequately complete the job.

CHAPTER 6 | INCREASE WORK DOSAGE

When the pressure to address many tasks leads to reducing the scope of work when performing each task, causing them to frequently return for further work.

CHAPTER 7 | STANDARDIZE TO SCALE

When too often work carried out by less experienced workers falls short, necessitates rework, and poses challenges to scaling without compromising work quality.

CHAPTER 8 | SYNCHRONIZE RESORUCES AND ACTIVITIES

When team members prioritize tasks based on local considerations, which are often not aligned with global priorities, thereby causing delays that are typically discovered in later stages of the project.

CHAPTER 9 | AGGREGATE AND MANAGE TIME BUFFERS

When the common perception that there aren't enough buffers leads team members to add whatever buffers they can to each task in the project. This approach wastes the very buffers needed to handle critical disruptions and uncertainty.

CHAPTER 10 | POOL RESOURCES

When resources are segmented to specific projects, shortages arise where demand is high, while surpluses build up where they are underutilized. This rigidity reduces flexibility and slows overall project flow.

Note that several obstacles may prevail in your environment, and you may very well need to integrate several of the solutions described herein.

Chapter 11 contains valuable warnings on what NOT to do, to enable you to focus and avoid wasting your time and resources.

When reviewing the obstacles to flow, you will most likely identify some that are more prevalent in your environment. You should identify the first obstacle to tackle and establish a corresponding mechanism to restrict WIP and improve flow. Then, determine how to further speed up flow by tackling other obstacles methodically. For example, you may decide to first triage the projects, as there are many low-value projects in the system that hinder the delivery of high-value ones. Next, you can work on full-kitting the selected projects or synchronizing their activities to further speed up their delivery. Alternatively, you may determine that bad multitasking is the major obstacle and set a restriction on the open work to reduce it. Then, you can increase the work dosages of selected projects, and so on.

Once you have tackled the dominant obstacles to flow in your operation, you should determine which buffers you need and where to place them. Remember, even with significant improvements to flow, some level of uncertainty and variability always remains. Reality is highly dynamic, and unanticipated disruptions may cause projects to be delayed. This is why buffers are always needed. If we fail to use buffers correctly, the stress on the people working on the projects may impel them to revert back to bad old practices that perpetuate vicious cycles. You should ensure that the buffers are aggregated and that they protect the Critical Chain.[3] Applying a mechanism to monitor the rate at which we progress on the Critical Chain versus the buffer consumption can provide an additional

---

[3]Additional information on Critical Chain will be provided in chapter 8 on setting a project plan. Also, if you're not familiar with the Critical Chain concept, there are plenty of online resources available for you to explore.

layer of protection since you will receive early warnings that the project is at high risk and can take remedial actions in time.

HOW TO CAUSE THE CHANGE?

Even good solutions to the right problems can fail in execution, often because they were not introduced properly to the organization. Instead of creating harmony, the manner in which they are introduced can create tension and conflicts. The following guidelines can help you to effectively introduce the solutions described in this book.

1 | Define the improvement goal: baseline and expected level of performance

● Performance can be measured by the number of projects completed within a certain time frame, speeding up the completion of key projects, meeting commitments to the customers, reducing the number of iterations, or some sort of productivity metric, such as the ratio of projects completed to the resources spent.

● The key is to define the improvement goal, so it clearly addresses the main challenges in the organization. Achieving the improvement goal should be considered a major success by both internal and external stakeholders.

● Ensure that the improvement goal is set high enough to compel the team to examine the deeply rooted practices in their operation. Low-bar objectives may feel safe but will not impel us to challenge inertia. To avoid stakeholders' resistance, explain that the goal is initially set high to force an examination of current operations and to develop game-changing solutions. It will not be set as a commitment until the solutions are proven effective by the team. In some cases, a Proof of Concept (POC) may be needed to alleviate concerns with setting high-bar goals. See the following chapters for further guidance.

● The improvement goal can be established collaboratively with managers responsible for project delivery and key stakeholders who are or can represent customers (those who order the work and receive the value). Typically, these goals need the explicit support of top management to set the stage for change.

2 | Establish a project flow committee and implementation team

● The project flow committee should be composed of key stakeholders who will be critical to the approval of the changes.

- The implementation team should consist of individuals responsible for designing and executing the changes.

- Be sure to include the managers who have the responsibility and authority to design, approve, and implement the solutions agreed upon between the members of the project flow committee and the implementation team.

3 | Have the committee and team members read the book *Goldratt's Rules of Flow* by Efrat Goldratt-Ashlag

- It is recommended to spread the reading and implementation over time. For example, ask team members to read one or two chapters each week.

- Discuss the chapters with the team. Is the obstacle to flow relevant to their environment? How can they tell? How to address it?

- Use this manual to guide the discussions and reach practical conclusions and solutions.

4 | Implement the solutions gradually

- The implementation steps should sequence the solutions that remove the obstacles to flow, starting with the dominant ones.

- It is better to focus on a limited number of changes that can be implemented quickly and achieve good results.

- Each implementation step must generate enough impact to create momentum for further changes.

- Evaluate the results continually to verify if the solution for the current obstacle should be further developed, expanded to more sections of the organization, or if it is time to move on to the next obstacle.

- As you implement the solutions, verify that you address measurement challenges and other issues that may stand in the way. See the following chapters for specific examples.

5 | Evaluate tactics to strengthen and leverage the solutions

- Once the new practices are proven to yield desired results, evaluate together with the team how to strengthen and systematize the solution. Now is the time to consider adding resources, restructuring the organization, setting specific metrics, providing additional training, collecting certain data, utilizing technology to automate the new processes, and reevaluating the growth strategy (e.g., the type of projects to be introduced).

- As you become successful in improving project performance, think how to leverage the new capabilities. Evaluate how completing more projects faster can be used for generating more business, creating a competitive edge, or delighting customers with extraordinary service.

6 | Beware of inertia

- Ensure the organization deploys sufficient buffers to accommodate growth or changes to the scope of work. If these buffers are depleted and resources are greatly overloaded with work, it may derail operations, and the vicious cycles will reappear.

- When new members join the team or when there is a change in management, make sure part of their introduction includes an overview of the reasons for the changes made and the improvements attained. Sharing success stories and results is the engine of cultural change.

- Ensure that someone is responsible for monitoring compliance with the new practices.

- Never underestimate the power of inertia! Ensure that the organization is on a path of ongoing improvement by continually setting higher and higher goals.

Now it's time to explore the prevailing obstacles to flow and the best strategies to overcome them. Then, synthesize this knowledge and put it into action.

GO!

TRIAGE
THE PROJECTS

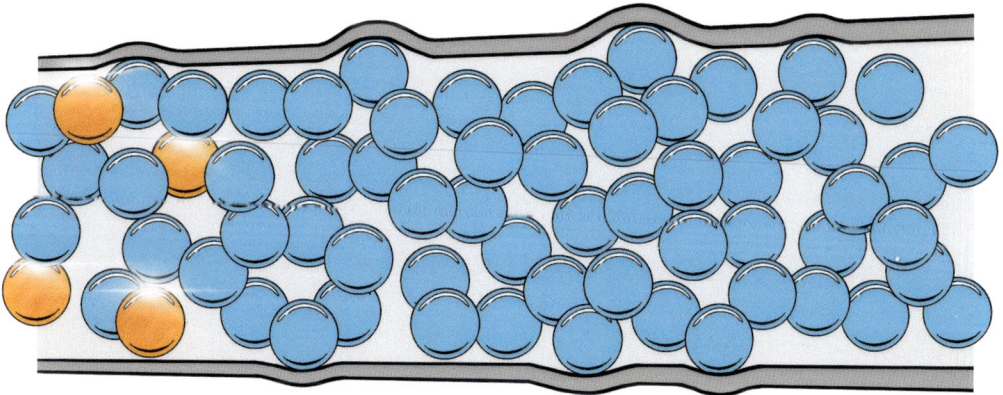

OBSTACLE TO FLOW

Excessive attention to low-value projects disrupts the focus on and progress of high-value projects, delaying their completion and compromising the scope and quality of their outcomes.

EXAMPLES

IT portfolio of projects in a bank. Like many organizations, banks are increasingly deploying digital transformation initiatives. Digital platforms enable more convenient customer interaction and optimize financial transactions in the bank. A large bank experienced dramatic growth in the budget allocated to developing and maintaining its digital assets. The demand for additional budget was constant while project cycle times continued to elongate. A thorough examination revealed that quantifying the expected Return on Investment (ROI) of many of its active digitization projects was quite challenging. Many IT projects aimed to automate operational processes to enhance the bank's efficiency as a means to reduce operating expenses. However, time savings translate into cost savings only if the bank spends less. It was not clear at all if there would be actual reductions in the workforce or overtime spending.

Another set of IT projects involved upgrading the bank's IT platform with the goal of enhancing customer experience. The examination scrutinized each IT project to verify that the new technology would, in fact, improve customer service and drive business growth. It was found that, in most cases, technology alone is insufficient and must be complemented by appropriate operational and business processes capable of leveraging the technology's capabilities. For instance, a significant budget was allocated to developing improved Customer Relationship Management (CRM) tools. One of these tools allowed customers to contact bankers via text messages. The tool was successfully developed; however, bankers were not adequately trained in what and how to communicate through this channel. This oversight left many customers dissatisfied, as their desire for more convenient and fast service was not met.

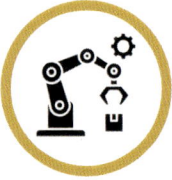

A manufacturer of production automation equipment maintained an extensive catalog of standard products. Due to intense competition in the market and the need to boost revenue, the sales team introduced a flood of highly customized machine orders that significantly deviated from the standard catalog items. These custom projects demanded substantially more engineering efforts and specialized components compared to the standard catalog items. Approving these custom projects disrupted the workflow for all orders and significantly eroded the company's overall profitability.

A company making automotive infotainment, which is integrated by car manufacturers as well as sold in the aftermarket, was developing a wide range of products that offered various combinations of features at different price points. These "features-to-price" combinations were advocated by the sales organization, which wanted to protect market share by matching the competition. While the development and marketing of these combinations required significant resources, they often resulted in products that were similar to those offered by competitors. This approach failed to create standout products that could make a significant impact on sales. Within the company's overall product development strategy, there were potentially valuable ideas that could have differentiated the company's products and provided high value to customers. Unfortunately, these ideas were often overlooked due to the overabundance of low-value trade-off projects.

THE CHALLENGE

In many work environments, people are overstretched, working on too many projects. While some of these projects can have a real impact on the organization's goal, many others fall short of expectations. Typically, various stakeholders and departments in the workplace initiate improvement projects. Since many of them are not in a position to impact the big picture and they are driven by local incentives, many of these projects aim to solve small, local problems that don't really help the company's main goal. Other projects could be valuable, but they need changes in core processes and coordination with other departments, which often does not happen. As a result, the organization's project portfolio often contains a plethora of low-value projects. When people work on projects that do not add much value, it diverts attention away from the more important projects. Because of this, even high-value projects tend to be completed late and do not achieve as much as expected. This situation is exacerbated when choosing projects becomes a source of conflict and politics, leading to even more unnecessary projects. In such scenarios, it becomes crucial to mitigate the impact of low-value projects on the successful delivery of high-impact ones. This is achieved through a rigorous project selection process that either excludes low-value projects or directs them toward operational paths that do not disrupt the progress of high-value projects. The real merit of the triage process lies in reducing the volume of active projects to free up resources and management attention to properly scope and deliver the selected high-value projects.

INDICATORS

How can you tell if there is a need to triage in your environment? Check if the following indicators are common issues faced by the team:

● CHALLENGES IN ALIGNING PROJECTS WITH BUSINESS GOALS

The link between projects and business goals is not straightforward, and considerable judgment is involved in picking the right projects. Consequently, many completed projects have little or no effect on the business goal.

● PRIORITIZATION ISSUES IN PROJECT SELECTION

The project portfolio selection process is highly politicized, with many different opinions, and creating alignment is challenging.

● RESOURCE SHORTAGES AND PROJECT DELAYS

Spreading resources across multiple projects slows down all projects. Consequently, cycle times inflate, leading to project delays and compromises on scope. The backlog of projects is very high and appears to keep growing.

● DECENTRALIZED PROJECT INITIATION

There is a delegation of authority, where people at various levels of the organization initiate projects aiming to improve performance.

● **FRUSTRATION AMONG TEAM MEMBERS AND MANAGEMENT.** Many projects do not add much value to the organization and are eventually abandoned. Workers are demotivated by the frequent switch in strategy and initiatives. Management is frustrated by the low ROI and underperformance in achieving goals.

THE VICIOUS CYCLE

Review the vicious cycle, in the following page, with your team to ensure alignment on the core challenge.

Various stakeholders in the organization are delegated with the responsibility to initiate projects aiming to improve performance (1). While the drive to enhance performance is welcome, when the responsibility to initiate projects across the organization is delegated, it often spawns a plethora of low-value projects. This is often the case because many of these projects tend to concentrate on local issues that do not significantly impact overall performance. Even when these projects have the potential to create substantial overall value, they often require changes in other departments or adjustments to the overall strategy, that go unaddressed (2). Evidently saying "No" to a manager trying to improve their performance is not easy. It may lead to the manager sometimes feeling dis-empowered. In other instances, it could lead to politics within the organization. Due to the vague criteria of project selection and the difficulty of saying "No" (3)," the organization finds itself under increasing pressure to initiate an ever-growing number of projects, a significant portion of which have low impact (4). With more projects in the pipeline, resources are stretched thin across many projects, significant number of which have low impact (5). Consequently, the management attention and resources allocated to low-value projects compromise the delivery of high-value projects (6). This results in chronic underperformance against the business goal (7), which sprouts even more projects aimed at rectifying the situation (1).

This vicious cycle is continuously reinforced by the ongoing pressure to improve on the business goals, often resulting in a large portfolio of projects where the high-value projects are not in focus.

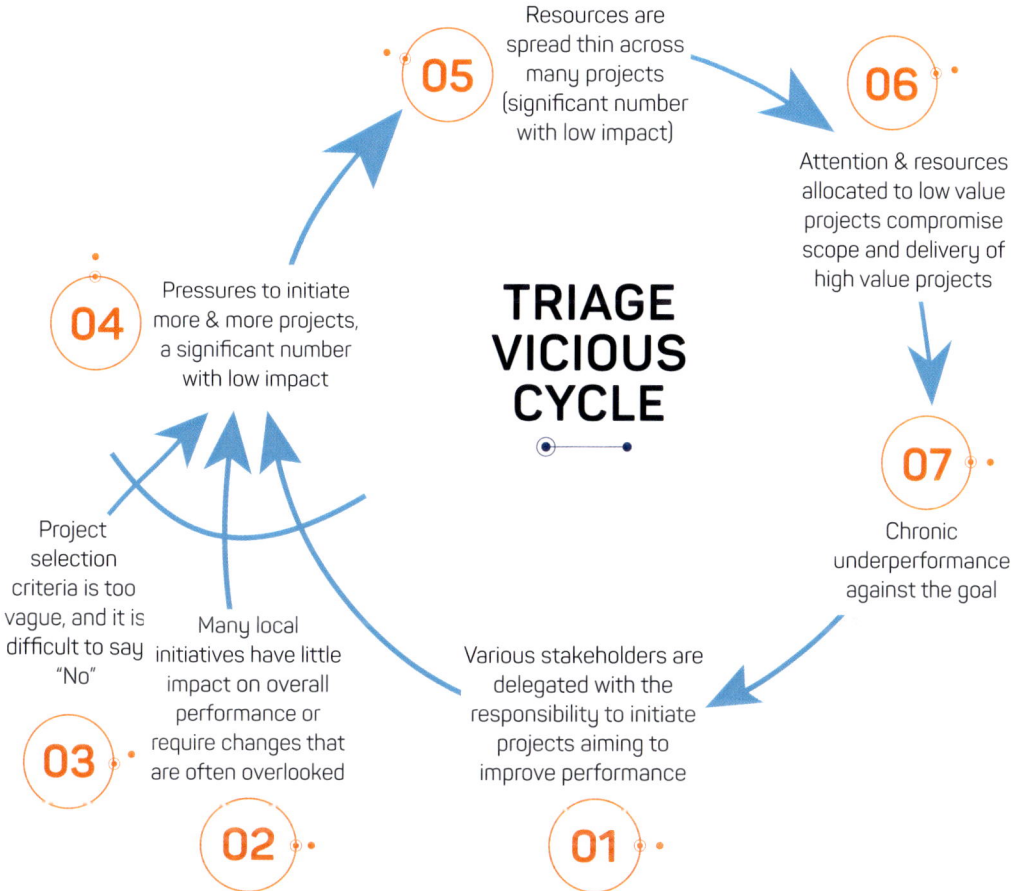

TRIAGE VICIOUS CYCLE

05 Resources are spread thin across many projects (significant number with low impact)

06 Attention & resources allocated to low value projects compromise scope and delivery of high value projects

04 Pressures to initiate more & more projects, a significant number with low impact

07 Chronic underperformance against the goal

03 Project selection criteria is too vague, and it is difficult to say "No"

02 Many local initiatives have little impact on overall performance or require changes that are often overlooked

01 Various stakeholders are delegated with the responsibility to initiate projects aiming to improve performance

THE SOLUTION

In environments where there is an overabundance of low-value projects, the key is to focus on improving the workflow of what really contributes to the organization's goals rather than just proliferating projects. There is no point in investing effort and money in accelerating the completion of projects when many of them are of low value. What is important is to get the high-value projects done faster and better. And this requires stopping the proliferation of low-value projects.

The pivotal change in this triage approach lies in centralizing the project selection process. This responsibility should rest with the leaders who are responsible for achieving the business objectives.

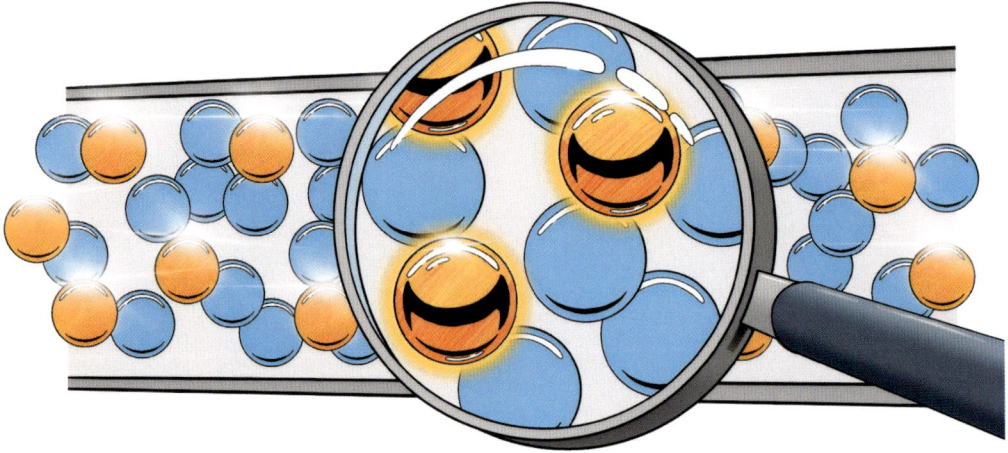

It is essential to have a well-defined "compass" that will guide the decision on which projects to initiate and their priority. By strengthening the process of prioritizing and starting projects, the volume of projects can be dramatically reduced and the scoping and completion rate of high-value projects significantly increased. Since these projects have a significant contribution, their acceleration helps the organization to achieve its goal.

PROJECT SELECTION & SCOPING

Determining which projects to focus on is carried out through the following steps:

STEP 1 | **DETERMINE THE BUSINESS GOAL.** When defining the business goal, ensure that it is quantifiable and achievable by the capabilities of the organization. Avoid the temptation to define inspiring goals that cannot be measured. Once you define the goal, verify its validity by defining associated goal units—units of measurement, such that generating more goal units indicates greater achievement of the goal.

STEP 2 | **DETERMINE THE GOAL "COMPASS".** This compass will help guide us to select the right projects. When the goal is clearly defined, the direct and quantifiable contribution of a project can be evaluated using a framework consisting of Throughput (T), Quality (Q), Operating Expenses (OE), and Inventory or Investment (I):

- Δ Throughput: the extent to which the project is attaining more of the goal in terms of goal units.

- Δ Operating Expense: the extent to which the project is reducing the ongoing cost of operating the business.

- Δ Investment: the extent to which the project reduces one-time costs.

Each project must undergo thorough scrutiny to determine its impact on Throughput, Quality, Operating Expenses, and Investment.

STEP 3 | SCOPE THE SELECTED PROJECTS FOR MAJOR SUCCESS. Reducing the number of active projects frees-up resources to properly scope and deliver the selected projects. To break the vicious cycle, it is not sufficient to select projects that have higher value than others. We have to ensure that the selected projects have a substantial rather than an incremental impact. Otherwise, the pressure to introduce many local projects will remain in effect. Remember, it is not about how many projects you are deploying. It is about their impact on the business goal. In reality, the sum of many local projects with incremental impact does not add up to a big impact on the business goal.

STEP 4 | ASSESS THE PROJECTS WITH RESPECT TO THEIR IMPACT ON RESOURCES, BUDGETS, AND TIMELINES. High-value projects can be prioritized based on the benefit they deliver relative to how much time, money, and effort they will consume.

STEP 5 | AS PROJECTS ARE SELECTED, ENSURE THAT THE NUMBER OF ACTIVE PROJECTS IS SIGNIFICANTLY REDUCED. So that the timeline for achieving the business goals is dramatically shortened. If this does not lead to a significant reduction in projects, the selection process is not strict enough.

STEP 6 | DIVERT NECESSARY LOW-VALUE PROJECTS. In situations where projects have a low impact on the overall business goal, it is not always possible to cancel them or neglect their completion. If faced with such a scenario, aim to minimize the disruption by allocating the least amount of necessary work to be expended on these projects. If possible, assign different people or schedule the work so that it does not conflict with high-priority projects. For more information on this approach, refer to Chapter 4 on segregating big and small tasks.

STEP 7 | **MONITOR AND PERFECT THE PROJECT SELECTION PROCESS.** As things change over time, the project portfolio may revert to an overabundance of low-value projects. This may happen because of compromises made in the selection process, or because some active projects are no longer relevant, and their value is diminished or lost. To prevent interference with the progress of high-value projects, it is recommended to conduct regular reviews of the value associated with the projects currently in the portfolio.

Let us consider some examples of applying the above steps:

IT portfolio of projects in a bank. A primary area of the bank's operations involved offering mortgages. When the management team ran the Triage process, they first defined the goal of achieving a substantial market share by delivering a superior, frictionless mortgage process to eligible customers. The bank assessed its IT project portfolio based on its impact on this goal. Initially, the bank considered continuing to invest in sophisticated CRM tools to track communication and progress. However, it became apparent that the additional investment did not provide additional value to customers. To ensure that the CRM tools delivered high value toward the goal, the team decided to address the mortgage processes and improve the customer experience. To start, the team mapped out the customer's journey in applying for and receiving a mortgage. This exercise aimed to find out how to provide eligible customers with a much faster and smoother process, reducing the need for back-and-forth interactions to obtain information. The decision was made to develop tools and processes that would enable customers to understand upfront the information required for obtaining a mortgage and to provide this information without even needing to visit the bank. Additionally, reminders would be sent to customers, using multiple modes of communication, about any missing information that was still required. Significant effort was put into simplifying the documents required from customers to streamline the process. Informing customers about the required information upfront also helped identify genuine business opportunities and process them more efficiently. Simply put, prospects who realize they do not meet the requirements while gathering this information do not proceed with an application. In consequence, the IT solutions complemented and facilitated the operational processes and marketing strategies, thereby maximizing the benefits of the new CRM technology.

A manufacturer of production automation equipment. This company accepted a surge of specialized orders for complex engineering products. However, due to increasing competition and the pressure to secure sales, this surge resulted in a noticeable drop in margins. These specialized orders also prolonged the delivery times for all orders, further reducing overall sales. To address these challenges and improve profitability, the management team initiated a Triage process aimed at increasing sales per operating expense. The process was implemented as follows:

● Customized orders were only accepted if they met a certain threshold of profit margin (gross contribution) relative to the operating expense involved.

● The team identified a few customized orders that had the potential to appeal to a much larger market segment. They then developed a plan to proactively promote these product variations to relevant customers. This approach made customized orders more standardized, allowing the company to service these customers with lower operating expenses.

● A platform was developed to configure different customized products using common modules. This enabled the company to control the level of operating expense involved in delivering customized products in a timely manner.

A company making automotive infotainment. The proliferation of product development initiatives aimed at creating a wide range of product variations at different price points did not result in any truly differentiating products. The focus was primarily on reacting to sales requests to match competitors' offerings rather than addressing customers' needs. Consequently, management made the decision to filter out low-value projects that would have a marginal impact to sales; instead, it emphasized the development of products that could effectively address significant limitations for customers. As part of this shift, the company decided to prioritize the development of a floating infotainment system with a much larger screen than those typically installed by automotive original equipment manufacturers (OEMs). This system was specifically designed to seamlessly integrate with most car systems, offering car owners the benefits of a substantially larger screen.

Additionally, the company established strong partnerships with car dealerships to offer these systems as an aftermarket option to customers purchasing new cars or seeking services for their current vehicles.

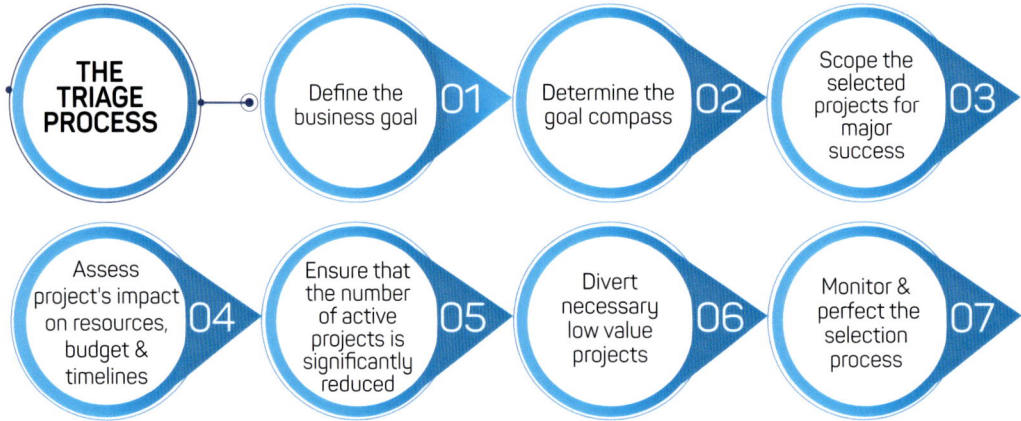

THE TRIAGE PROCESS	Define the business goal	01	Determine the goal compass	02	Scope the selected projects for major success	03
	Assess project's impact on resources, budget & timelines	04	Ensure that the number of active projects is significantly reduced	05	Divert necessary low value projects	06	Monitor & perfect the selection process	07

HOW TO CAUSE THE CHANGE?

There are several obstacles we need to overcome when applying Triage:

● Many stakeholders may have projects that are close to their heart, and are concerned they might be canceled in the triage exercise.

● Leadership's bandwidth is limited; it is too busy managing the high number of active projects.

● People may be concerned that centralizing the project selection decisions can hurt their metrics.

● The sunk cost fallacy often prevails, wherein management hesitates to terminate low-value projects due to the substantial investments already made. This obstacle persists even when it becomes evident that anticipated results will not materialize.

To significantly improve the situation, the change has to be drastic. People have to realize that the business pain is intense, and continuing with the current path will risk the business goal. Hence there is not much to lose. This realization can be leveraged to create buy-in for dramatic action as follows:

1 | Buy-in of team: Bring the stakeholders of the portfolio together to secure buy-in on the fact that the current situation is untenable. If nothing changes, the business goals will not be achieved, and everyone will lose. The alternative is to make careful decisions and drastically limit the active projects. It is important to highlight to the team that this drastic reduction will speed up the execution of projects with the highest contribution to the business goals. In addition, the team can be reassured that the deep dive into projects' evaluation using T, Q, I, and OE will help create a structured, correct way to make centralized portfolio decisions.

2 | Establish the forum: When the responsibility for achieving the goal is delegated, it leads to a proliferation of lower-value improvement projects across the organization. Many projects will not receive adequate resources and management attention and will fail to achieve significant results. Move from distributed decision-making to centralized portfolio management by getting top leadership involved in the decision-making process. Ensure that everyone understands that the forum members have a global and holistic view of the entire system so that projects will yield real value. Implement the right meeting, agenda, and process to make portfolio decisions.

3 | Formalize the criteria: Articulate the decision-making criteria and get consensus. It is important to articulate the criteria before the process of project selection commences. It helps establish objectivity and reduce politics in the selection process.

Estimating the impact on T, Q, I, and OE for every project will require us to clarify the goal and the scope of each project.

4 | Make decisions to reduce the number of active projects: Ensure that applying the project selection criteria will, in fact, substantially reduce the number of active projects.

5 | Improve the flow in execution: A benefit of a dramatic reduction in projects is accelerated project completion. This acceleration will not happen by itself; resource concentration (now possible due to the reduction in number of active projects), project plans, and execution practices will have to be changed to achieve the requisite results.

6 | Measure operational performance and business results: Implement the right metrics, that align with the new framework, into the company practices.

The examples below illustrate some of the key steps involved in executing Triage:

In an **IT Portfolio**, the responsibility for initiating projects lies with the various departments and business units. The departments and business units control the budget and treat the IT group as a cost center in delivering services. Triaging projects requires a common forum, encompassing the IT, the funding departments, and top leadership of the company to select projects in accordance with well-defined criteria. Doing so centralizes decision-making and ensures that the selected projects deliver true value. The business units should be measured in accordance with the project selection decisions so that they make the necessary changes to achieve the business goals.

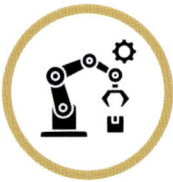

For the **custom equipment manufacturer**, the change in pricing and offering has to be made by the top leadership of the company. The goals and targets of the salespeople have to be aligned with the portfolio strategy. Salespeople should be measured in a way that promotes the selling of highly customized products only at premium prices and standard products at competitive prices. This change will align the behaviors of the sales team to the portfolio strategy.

For the **maker of automotive infotainment**, the change of making a product with a large floating screen, which would be offered as a dealer option, required top management to make this decision and get the buy-in of the sales organization. To achieve this buy-in, the company engaged the sales organization early on by creating a product catalog that helped visualize the product and its benefits. The sales catalog was shared with dealers, who could then test it with customers to get an indication of the excitement the product engendered.

This advanced testing helped refine the product requirements and get the buy-in of the sales organization on prioritizing this product while deprioritizing the many projects aimed at matching the competitors feature-cost trade-offs. The buy-in from the sales organization was critical in promoting this product in the market once it was ready.

GUIDING QUESTIONS FOR GROUP DISCUSSION & IMPLEMENTATION

Follow these guiding questions to facilitate a discussion with your team on triaging your project portfolio:

THE NEED TO TRIAGE

1 Are there high-value projects in the pipeline that need to be expedited for maximal benefit?

2 Are the resources needed to expedite these high-value projects currently held by less impactful assignments?

3 How relevant are the list of indicators and the vicious cycle?

SETTING UP TO TRIAGE

4 Who should be part of the committee responsible for defining project selection criteria and evaluating both active and future projects?

5 What business goal are we aiming to attain? What are the goal units indicating greater attainment of the goal?

LET'S TRIAGE

6 Considering ΔT, ΔQ, ΔOE, and ΔI, which projects should we focus on?

7 Are the selected projects scoped correctly for major success?

8 Is it possible to terminate and decline low-value projects? If not, how can they be managed to avoid interference with high-value project execution?

9 How can we obtain buy-in of key stakeholders? Is there a need to change metrics to ensure the right behaviors?

VALIDATION

10 Using the selection criteria, has the number of active projects been reduced enough to accelerate high-value projects?

11 Do the selected projects provide sufficient results?

REDUCE BAD MULTITASKING

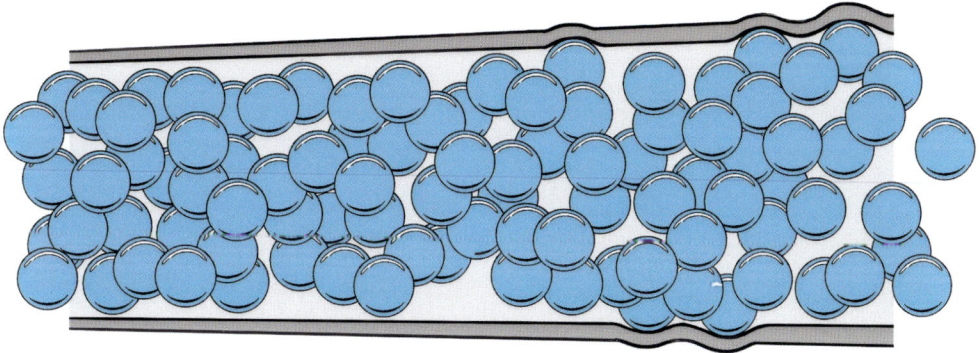

OBSTACLE TO FLOW

Team members often switch across projects and tasks before completing them, significantly increasing lead times, and reducing productivity.

EXAMPLES

IT Departments in Large Corporations. IT departments, especially in large corporations, are prime examples of environments where multitasking is prevalent. IT professionals frequently juggle numerous tasks, including maintaining, updating, and troubleshooting IT infrastructure, while also deploying new technologies. The necessity to switch among tasks, such as responding to urgent technical support tickets while implementing assignments like software updates or cybersecurity measures, can lead to delays and errors.

Heavy Engineering Projects. An engineering firm specializes in producing equipment, such as various high-pressure vessels, for chemical process plant industries and the nuclear power sector. Its projects have long lead times and require extensive engineering efforts during the requirement gathering, design, and production support stages. Generally, the same engineers are responsible for managing a project through these phases. They frequently multitask across projects at various stages. Delays, urgent work, and reworking tasks are common at the company.

Design Department. A company that makes sports clothes for global brands has a design team that is overwhelmed. The designers manage multiple orders in the pipeline alongside new design specifications requested by different customers. Changing priorities and waiting for customer feedback slowed progress, resulting in longer lead times than customers expected.

THE CHALLENGE

Bad multitasking is one of the most common obstacles to flow. It refers to those occasions when team members switch across projects and tasks without completing them. Rather than focus and finish one task at a time, team members work on tasks in intervals, repeatedly shifting back and forth. This mode of operation significantly increases the time required to complete each task. Moreover, shifting of focus from one task to another, results in constant context switching that wastes considerable time as team members need to reorient themselves with each switch. This constant context switching inevitably gives rise to mistakes, which likely necessitate rework and further prolong lead times. The effects of hectic, bad multitasking exacerbate the situation exponentially when different team members, all engaged in multitasking, must coordinate their efforts to make progress.

Just setting task priorities is insufficient to reduce the impact of bad multitasking in such environments. One of the reasons team members multitask is that priorities constantly shift across tasks and projects. A more effective way to significantly reduce the impact of bad multitasking is to limit the number of tasks that team members can work on simultaneously. The success of this strategy depends on the organization's discipline in sticking to this limit, allowing team members to focus and finish their work.

INDICATORS

How can we tell that hectic, bad multitasking prevails in our environment? Determine whether the following indicators are common issues faced by your team:

● **TASKS TAKE MUCH LONGER TO COMPLETE.** In the scenario described in the following figure, the same person is working on three tasks—A, B, and C. In the first row, the three tasks are performed sequentially without multitasking. After completing one task, the person starts working on the next one. In the second row, the person multitasks across the tasks. Note the effect of multitasking on the lead time to complete tasks A and B. The third row indicates the realistic situation where the person needs to reorient themselves when switching back to a task they had not worked on for a while. In context switches, each task frequently takes much longer to complete.

THE IMPACT OF BAD MULTITASKING ON LEAD TIMES

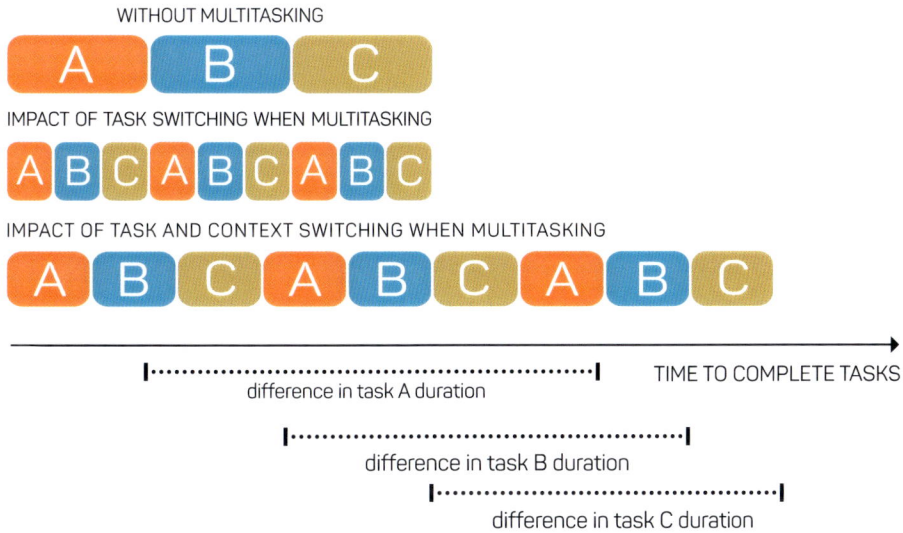

WITHOUT MULTITASKING

A B C

IMPACT OF TASK SWITCHING WHEN MULTITASKING

A B C A B C A B C

IMPACT OF TASK AND CONTEXT SWITCHING WHEN MULTITASKING

A B C A B C A B C

TIME TO COMPLETE TASKS

difference in task A duration

difference in task B duration

difference in task C duration

● **IMPOSSIBLE TO FOCUS ON AND FINISH A TASK BEFORE BEING PULLED TO ANOTHER TASK.** Team members constantly tackle switching priorities. They are pulled by different stakeholders and instructed to stop whatever they are working on and switch to work on different tasks. Their frustration grows as everyone is breathing down their neck. This continuous interruption of work frustrates them as they struggle to accomplish anything substantial. The pressure from all sides and the feeling of being part of a relentless "rat race" severely impact their motivation and overall morale.

● **RESOURCES ARE NOT AVAILABLE WHEN NEEDED.** Team members struggle to coordinate with each other when everyone is caught up in hectic multitasking. They often don't wait until others become available and switch to other tasks to keep going. For example, in the figure below, person A is busy and not available for person B; B switches to another task; A becomes available, but at that time, B is busy with another task. Now, A switches to yet another task, and B becomes available... Such ineffective multitasking cycles significantly prolong the completion of tasks.

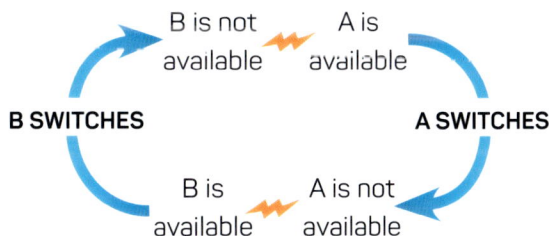

B is not available   A is available

B SWITCHES   **A SWITCHES**

B is available   A is not available

● **THE BACKLOG OF TASKS KEEPS GROWING AND URGENCIES ARE COMMON**. Multitasking increases the lead time to complete tasks while new tasks keep joining the task queue. The pressure to get things done grows. Important matters become urgent. Priorities progress from red to red hot and then to "drop everything and do it now."

● **KEY PEOPLE ARE OVERLOADED.** The pressure to multitask is exceptionally high on key people, whose work capacity is limited, and demand for their attention is high. Often, this leads to high stress and burnout affecting their overall productivity and well-being, and potentially leading to a higher turnover rate.

● **HIGH REWORK AND PRODUCTIVITY LOSS.** The pressure to release tasks from the backlog for execution without adequate preparation, the limited availability of key people, the constant context switching, all give rise to many mistakes, requiring rework. When tasks loop back for rework it adds additional workload on already overburdened workers and the backlog keeps growing.

THE VICIOUS CYCLE

Review the vicious cycle with your team to ensure alignment on the core challenge. When demand for products and services spikes the workload often exceeds the team's capacity, which remains limited (1). This mismatch results in a growing backlog of tasks (2). At this point, tasks languishing in the task queue become urgent, with various stakeholders demanding their completion. Priorities shift frequently, sometimes dictated by who clamors the loudest (3). Team members, attempting to appease multiple stakeholders, oscillate across tasks. Bad multitasking becomes routine (4). It takes longer to complete a task when performed piecemeal in multiple intervals. The frequent task switches require additional time as each context switch demands extra time for reorientation. This often gives rise to errors, necessitating rework, which further increases the workload and lead times. The challenge of coordination with other multitasking members makes it impossible to finish tasks in one go. Lead times grow beyond expectations (5). Since it takes longer to complete tasks, while new tasks keep arriving, the backlog of tasks continuously grows (2). Thus, we get trapped in a vicious cycle, as shown in the following figure. If only we could simply reduce the workload or hire more people. Unfortunately, if it were easy to do, we would likely not have reached this reality.

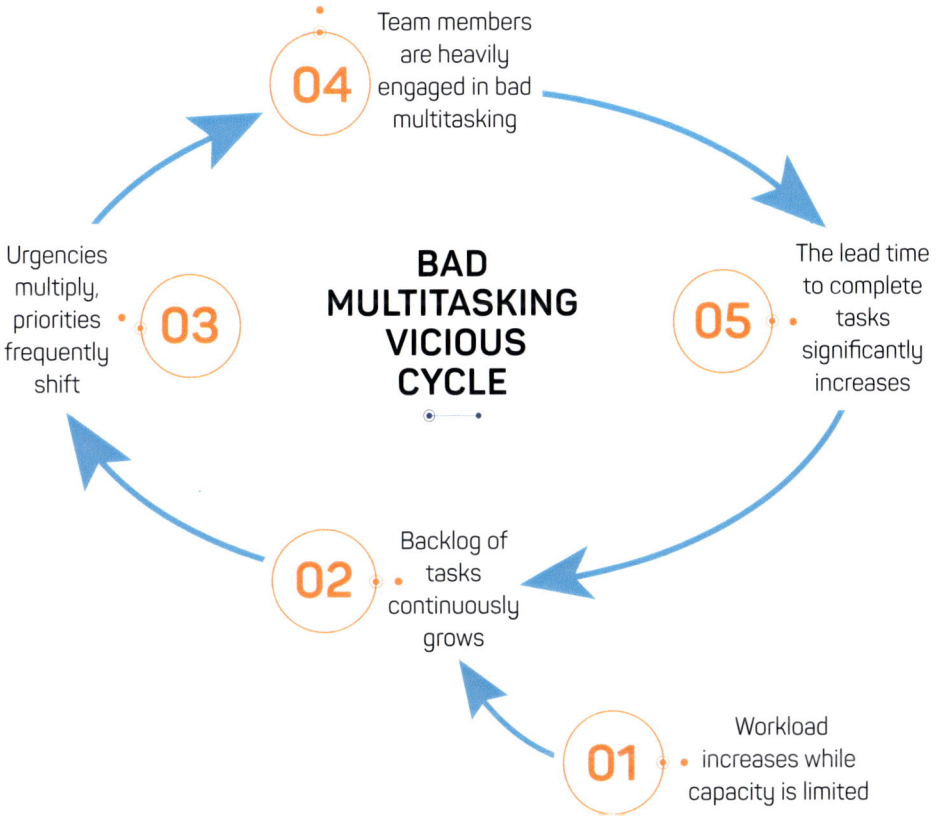

BAD MULTITASKING VICIOUS CYCLE

- **04** Team members are heavily engaged in bad multitasking
- **05** The lead time to complete tasks significantly increases
- **03** Urgencies multiply, priorities frequently shift
- **02** Backlog of tasks continuously grows
- **01** Workload increases while capacity is limited

THE SOLUTION

When bad multitasking is common, we feel pressure to address tasks piling up in the task queue. This shifts our focus away from efficiently completing tasks in progress. We aim to start more tasks as soon as possible and devote less time to each one before switching to another. However, to improve the workflow, we must reduce multitasking across projects and tasks and adopt a "focus and finish" mindset.

The following figure illustrates the relation between the number of open tasks, Work In Process (WIP) and the inefficiencies in the workflow. On the left side of the curve, WIP is low, some resources may be idle, and productivity is lost. As we add more tasks and swing to the right side of the curve, team members are compelled to multitask, lead times increase, and productivity drops. Cutting down the WIP levels from the red dot to the green dot breaks this pendulum swing and dramatically improves the workflow.

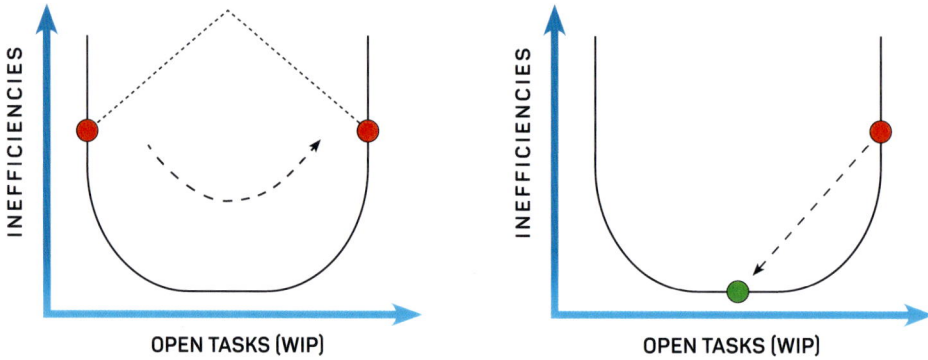

Impact of reducing WIP on tasks completion

RESTRICTING OPEN PROJECTS / TASKS

WIP levels can be effectively reduced by setting limits on the number of active tasks per person or department. This approach automatically serves to cut down on multitasking across projects and tasks, leading to earlier completion times.

The heavy engineering company initially chose to limit the number of tasks that are assigned to each engineer. Previously, only 25% of projects were completed on time, but by reducing the number of open tasks, engineers were able to accelerate task completion. As a result, the company improved the on-time performance of projects from 25% to 50%, even as the project load increased (effectively doubling productivity). Despite this progress, the performance was still deemed unsatisfactory. Management was still overly occupied with renegotiating delivery times and addressing customer complaints. The subsequent initiative involved limiting the overall number of projects in progress, which directly accelerated project completion. This approach required careful management of customer expectations, as it delayed the launch of some projects. By restricting the number of open projects, the company achieved an on-time delivery rate of approximately 90%.

The substantial improvement in on-time delivery fostered greater trust and satisfaction among customers. Engineers reported experiencing less stress and higher engagement, as they could focus on completing tasks without constant interruptions.

The sports apparel design department faced significant overload when managing multiple orders in the pipeline alongside new design specifications requested by customers. To address this challenge, the department head stopped allocating design work to designers as soon as it entered the system. She limited the number of open jobs each designer could work on and allocated new jobs only upon completion of existing ones. This simple adjustment led to a remarkable 40% increase in productivity, measured by jobs completed per month.

A similar strategy was adopted in **the IT department,** where the number of open job tickets assigned to code developers was significantly reduced. Tasks were allocated as team members became available after completing other jobs. Considering the urgent nature of some IT tasks, the department kept a sufficient pool of workers to handle urgent matters to avoid overwhelming the team with multitasking. To ensure there were enough available workers for urgent tasks, the company made sure team members had a wide range of skills to meet diverse IT work.

As the examples above show, it's better to gather tasks in a general task queue and wait to launch a task until the requisite resources are freed rather than assign them to specific people as soon as the tasks arrive. This approach means tasks in the general queue can be addressed more quickly by the next available team member. Moreover, assigning tasks to specific individuals as they arrive often leads to multitasking, which reduces efficiency.

In situations where only specific people can handle certain tasks, maintaining a dedicated task queue becomes necessary. This approach is naturally less efficient than using a general queue and can lead to more delays as the workload increases and the task queue builds up. To improve workflow, management needs to consider cross training people to offload the ones that are overloaded.

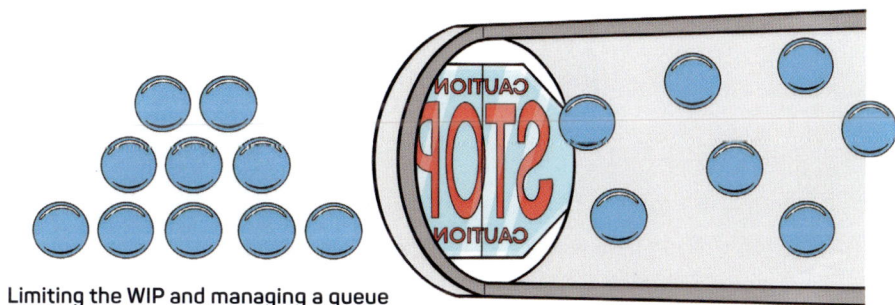

Limiting the WIP and managing a queue

THE WIP BOARD

A valuable tool for controlling and monitoring work release is the WIP board. This visual management tool consists of several columns that clearly depict the number of tasks in progress, those assigned to wait in a queue, those on hold waiting for missing inputs, and those completed. The WIP board facilitates the visualization of the state of work and its restrictions and can be applied at both the individual and department levels.

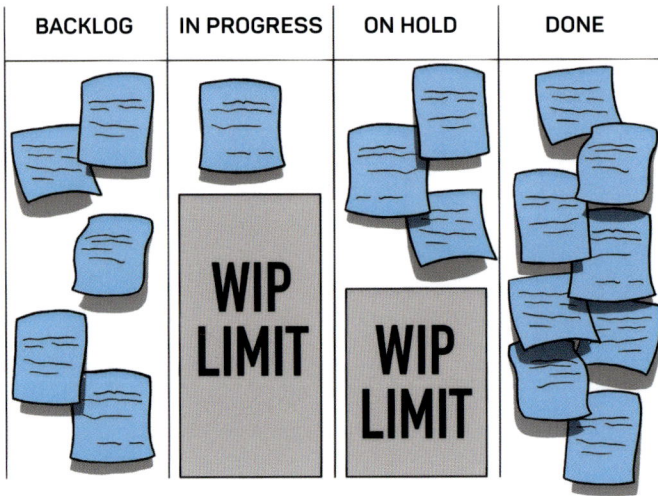

Once the WIP boards are set up, the team should implement a daily 20-minute stand-up meeting. The meeting objective is to ensure that the WIP restrictions are met, issues are identified and resolved quickly, and tasks in queues are readied for execution.

HOW TO DETERMINE THE RIGHT WIP LEVEL?

Here are several guidelines to help determine the right WIP in terms of the number of active tasks and projects:

● THE NUMBER OF TASKS PER PERSON SHOULD BE LIMITED

A task is a unit of work that people can start and finish in one continuous time interval. As a general guideline, workers should not have more than one active task. Tasks that have issues will be on hold. The focus should be on the speed of resolving issues. Don't let tasks on hold accumulate.

● FREEZING PROJECTS TO REDUCE MULTITASKING

Consider temporarily halting 25% to 50% of active projects.

In cases where projects are utilizing the same resources throughout the project, simply cut the number of open projects.

In cases where different project phases use different resources, halting projects can still leave certain resources tied up in heavy multitasking. This occurs because the remaining active projects may involve phases that overload certain people with excessive work. To manage this, implement a simple template project plan that clearly outlines each project phase and specifies the required workers. Then, begin assigning workers to the highest-priority projects to ensure their timely completion. As people are allocated to accelerate prioritized projects, we inevitably reach projects that cannot be adequately staffed. These will be halted and moved to the project queue, effectively reducing WIP for each phase. Our goal should be to reduce the overall number of active projects by 25% to 50%, although this reduction might vary across different phases.

● PRIORITIZING PROJECTS FOR COMPLETION

Focus on completing projects that are closest to completion first. Allocate all necessary resources to ensure the project or the phase progresses quickly. This ensures that we achieve a stable state of low WIP.

When halting projects and reallocating workers to active ones, some workers may remain idle. These workers can then help complete all preparations for the next projects in the project queue (see Chapter 5 on full-kitting). Such preparation can accelerate the execution of these projects once workers become available and are activated. At this stage, implementing a "one-out-one-in" rule can help control the WIP magnitude of projects and establish a common mindset to focus and finish tasks and projects.

● MONITOR THE PROGRESS OF TASKS TO CONTINUOUSLY IMPROVE FLOW

To ensure a smooth workflow there are two crucial factors to monitor:

1 QUEUE MONITORING. Keep a close eye on the task queue, including both the general queue and the queues allocated to workers. If wait time in the queue grows, it indicates that tasks are taking longer to complete than planned. Investigate potential obstacles to flow that may be causing the delays. This could include still too high allocated WIP, leading to bad multitasking or other flow obstacles explained in this book, such as incomplete kits, proliferation of low-value projects, or high mix of big and small tasks. Once these obstacles are addressed, in case the queue length still remains high, it may be necessary to consider adding resources to increase capacity.

2 ACTIVE TASK STATUS MONITORING. Regularly monitor specific assigned tasks that are on hold awaiting certain inputs, such as information, decisions, or authorizations. Additionally, tasks may be on hold while waiting for a certain resource to become available. Such monitoring is crucial for resolving stuck tasks promptly and for conducting future statistical analysis to identify sources of flow disruption. To support this monitoring, establish a timeframe for the expected completion of tasks. Tasks that take longer to complete will be highlighted as having issues (and probably should have been highlighted as "on hold"). For further details refer to the Chapter 9 - Aggregate and Manage Time Buffers.

HOW TO CAUSE THE CHANGE

As we plan to restrict open work and freeze projects, we should expect that various stakeholders will raise several concerns:

● **IDLE RESOURCES.** When freezing projects, it's possible that some people will have nothing to do for a period of time.

● **POTENTIAL PROJECT DELAYS.** Freezing projects can delay the start of some projects. Both project managers and top management may be nervous that these projects will not be completed on time.

● **URGENT TASKS AND CHANGES IN PRIORITIES.** Some stakeholders may insist on keeping the flexibility to change priorities and task assignments.

To address the above concerns, it is essential to involve all critical stakeholders (like sales account managers, department heads, project managers, etc.) in the decision-making process of which projects to keep active and which to put on hold. It is useful to utilize exercises with stakeholders in order to demonstrate the benefits of reducing bad multitasking. There are plenty of video clips and exercises you can find online to engage your team and demonstrate the negative impacts of bad multitasking.

Sometimes it is necessary to implement a POC to gain confidence and buy-in. Designing the POC involves careful planning and execution to test the effectiveness of reducing multitasking. Here's a step-by-step approach for the POC:

1 IDENTIFY A REPRESENTATIVE AREA. Select a small but representative area within the current process where you can implement multitasking reduction. This area should be indicative of the broader system and its challenges. Make sure the selected area for POC has a set of resources and projects that are somewhat isolated from other resources that are not part of the POC.

2 DEFINE SUCCESS CRITERIA. Clearly define the success criteria for the POC. Determine the specific increase in throughput that will be considered a success.

3 IMPLEMENT WIP REDUCTION. Cut the WIP and develop a mechanism to make work visible (such as the WIP board). Remember to hold the stand-up meeting to accelerate issue identification and resolution.

4 EVALUATE THE PILOT. Evaluate the results against the predefined success criteria. Determine if the multitasking reduction led to the desired increase in throughput and if any other positive or negative effects were observed.

5 DEFINE NEXT STEPS FOR EXPANSION. Based on the POC results, address any observed negatives and determine the feasibility and potential benefits of expanding the WIP reduction to the project level. Establish a clear plan for the next phase of implementation.

By following this POC format, you can assess the impact of reducing multitasking, validate its benefits, and pave the way for further implementation throughout the operation.

In certain cases, restricting open projects raises additional concerns that need special consideration:

● **CUSTOMER EXPECTATIONS FOR PROGRESS.** Managing customer expectations is crucial. Customers may monitor their projects closely and be concerned if people are not working on their projects. Naturally, we should explain the reasoning behind controlling the work released into the system. However, it may take a while before the customers experience better performance and gain confidence in the new system.

● **IDENTIFYING RISKS AND EMERGENT SCOPE.** In some project environments, we uncover potential risks and emergent scope only when starting the project. Delaying the project start can lead to late discovery of such risks, and there may not be sufficient time to recover.

If you encounter such concerns in your environment, you may need to create a preliminary discovery phase before the project starts. This phase will focus on defining the scope and full-kit of the project before execution. It should focus on revealing the main uncertainty in the scope associated with the project. Conducting such a phase will also serve as a means to show customers that their project is being treated. Once this phase is complete, the project should commence only as per the WIP limit restriction rules.

GUIDING QUESTIONS FOR GROUP DISCUSSION & IMPLEMENTATION

Follow these guiding questions to facilitate a discussion with your team on reducing bad multitasking in your operation:

IDENTIFYING AREAS OF HECTIC MULTITASKING

1   Which team members are heavily engaged in bad multitasking? Look for:
Growing queues of tasks and projects
Longer task and project completion times
Constant rework
Burnout and fatigue suffered by team members

2   How relevant are the list of indicators and the vicious cycle?

SETTING UP WIP RESTRICTION

3   What is the desired completion time for high-priority projects? How many projects/ tasks should be active to get these high-priority projects completed on time?

4   When should work be assigned? Who should be responsible for this?

5   When should work be released and activated? Who should be responsible for this?

VALIDATION

6   Considering the WIP restriction, is multitasking significantly reduced and are tasks completed at a much faster rate?

If not, should we further restrict WIP? Should restrictions be imposed at the team members' task level or at the department's project level?

If yes, would further WIP restriction achieve even better results?

SUSTAINING THE RESULTS

7   How do you handle shifts in priorities of tasks and projects?

8   Who should be responsible for resolving issues in task execution?

9   How should we accelerate problem-solving and promptly address the tasks on hold?

SEGREGATE BIG
& SMALL TASKS

OBSTACLE TO FLOW

The same team members handle a mix of low-load and high-load jobs, ending up compromising on the delivery of all jobs.

EXAMPLES

At an **electrical equipment manufacturing company**, engineers are responsible for designing custom-made electrical cabinets for buildings, industry, infrastructure facilities, etc. These cabinets come in two categories: regular custom-made cabinets and highly customized cabinets. The regular custom-made cabinets are part of the standard product catalog. They are designed according to established templates and specifications, and the engineering team is well-versed in creating them efficiently. These cabinets require less time to design and are relatively straightforward. On the other hand, highly customized cabinets are unique and tailored to meet specific client requirements, for example, infrastructure or industrial projects and different structures with unique conditions. These cabinets deviate significantly from the standard designs, often involving unconventional layouts, additional safety features, etc. Designing these cabinets is a time-consuming and complex process. When an engineer is engaged in designing highly customized cabinets, the queue of regular jobs begins to grow, leading to prolonged lead times for those routine projects.

Pharma R&D scientists, engaged in a lengthy process of developing a new pharmaceutical formulation, often face interruptions from the production engineering team. These interruptions occur because the production engineers are working on designing a manufacturing process for other formulations and often need guidance from the scientists. These inquiries are vital for the engineers to proceed with designing the production process effectively. However, for the researchers, these interruptions can be disruptive to their core workflow, as they need to shift their focus from formulation development to addressing production-related questions and providing insights to aid in the process design.

Professionals working in the **accounting department** of a rapidly expanding firm must handle both low-load tasks (routine financial reporting, invoices, transaction processing, basic data entry, etc.) and supporting high-load responsibilities (critical financial analysis, budget planning, complex audits, etc.). As the company grows, the accounting team often struggles to manage the growing load of these diverse tasks. Low-load tasks occasionally queue up and wait for an available worker, thereby creating pressure to expedite them. High-load tasks are frequently interrupted by urgent low-load responsibilities. These patterns of multitasking compromise the accuracy and efficiency of all deliveries.

In a **software company**, the development team juggled various projects, ranging from major feature development to routine bug-fixing tasks and addressing user interface improvements. While smaller tasks were crucial for maintaining the software's overall quality and user experience, they often took a backseat to larger initiatives focused on developing exciting new features. As time passed, some of these low-load tasks began to accumulate and fall behind schedule, leading to user complaints and decreased satisfaction. The increasing pressure from various stakeholders to address these tasks resulted in ongoing interruptions and frequent changes to the development team's work schedule.

In a bustling **hospital** setting, doctors are primarily focused on delivering expert care to their patients, ensuring that their medical needs are met with precision and efficiency. However, the collaborative nature of healthcare often requires doctors to provide valuable input to colleagues treating admitted patients in different wards or departments. These inputs could include consultations, recommendations, or critical medical information. When doctors prioritize their core responsibilities of patient care, they may sometimes delay providing input to peers, unaware that this might cause unforeseen challenges in patient treatment and length of stay at the hospital.

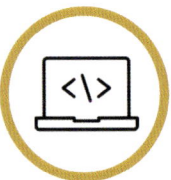

In **software development**, programmers often face a dilemma: balancing the need to participate in design and code reviews with the imperative of advancing new code development. These team reviews play a pivotal role in maintaining the quality and uniformity of the software under development. They offer a valuable opportunity to spot and resolve issues and ensure that the code is aligned with the project's objectives. However, these collaborative activities can consume considerable time, to the extent that developers have to work extra time to complete their personal coding.

THE CHALLENGE

As the above examples show, "Elephants and rabbits don't run together." In many work environments, team members are often required to handle both low-load jobs, and high-load jobs that consume significantly more of their capacity. When handling this mix of low and high-load jobs on a regular basis, two common issues tend to arise:

1 Low-load jobs often have to wait for specific workers to complete a high-load job. This increases their lead times, causes delays in meeting commitments, and mounting pressure to expedite these low-load tasks.

2 High-load jobs frequently face interruptions from low-load jobs, resulting in bad multitasking that adversely affects both the time and quality of high-load job deliveries.

To effectively address these challenges, especially when they reach an overwhelming level, it is essential to segregate low-load and high-load jobs. This can only be achieved by assigning them to different team members or scheduling them in separate predefined time slots.

INDICATORS

How can we tell if poor segregation is a prevailing obstacle in our environment? Determine if the following indicators are common issues faced by the team:

● **LONG QUEUE OF LOW-LOAD JOBS.** Poor segregation is often indicated by a significant backlog of low-load tasks waiting to be addressed by specific team members who are currently engaged in major assignments. Such a backlog can lead to increased lead times, delays, and eventually urgency to address these tasks.

● **CONSTANT INTERRUPTIONS.** When workers are frequently interrupted to answer questions or handle ongoing low-load tasks, it can prevent them from concentrating on their core activities. This constant shifting of focus suggests a lack of clear separation between different types of work.

● **WORKING OUTSIDE OFFICIAL HOURS.** One commonly observed effect of poor task segregation is the phenomenon of employees regularly extending their work hours beyond official work periods (e.g., evenings, weekends, early mornings) to focus on their long-term assignments, or go through the backlog of small tasks, without interruptions.

● **ESCALATION OF SMALL MATTERS.** When seemingly small but important issues escalate into crises due to neglect or delayed attention, it is a sign of poor segregation. This can result in a need for last-minute, high-pressure multitasking to resolve these crises.

● **HECTIC MULTITASKING.** The phenomenon of workers engaged in hectic multitasking, across high-load and low-load jobs, is indicative of poor segregation. This can negatively impact the quality and efficiency of their work.

THE VICIOUS CYCLE

Review the vicious cycle with your team to ensure alignment on the core challenge. In some cases, high-load jobs are the core activity for certain team members and therefore take priority (1). When this happens, these team members will naturally perform the high-load jobs at the expense of low-load tasks that are also on their plate (2). Essentially, this means that low-load tasks end up waiting for team members to become available, resulting in increased lead times (3). As the backlog of small tasks increases and lead times become significantly longer, customers or other stakeholders start exerting pressure to have their tasks addressed promptly (4). This mounting pressure eventually leads these low-load tasks to regularly disrupt progress on high-load assignments (5). Team members are then caught in hectic multitasking, struggling to balance their workload (6). Consequently, this leads to delays in completing major tasks, often accompanied by quality issues and the need for rework (7). As a result, team members will then revert to giving priority to the high-load tasks and perform them at the expense of low-load tasks (2).

This continuous swing between high- and low-load tasks, perpetuates inefficiency and quality issues, as well as burnout and fatigue.

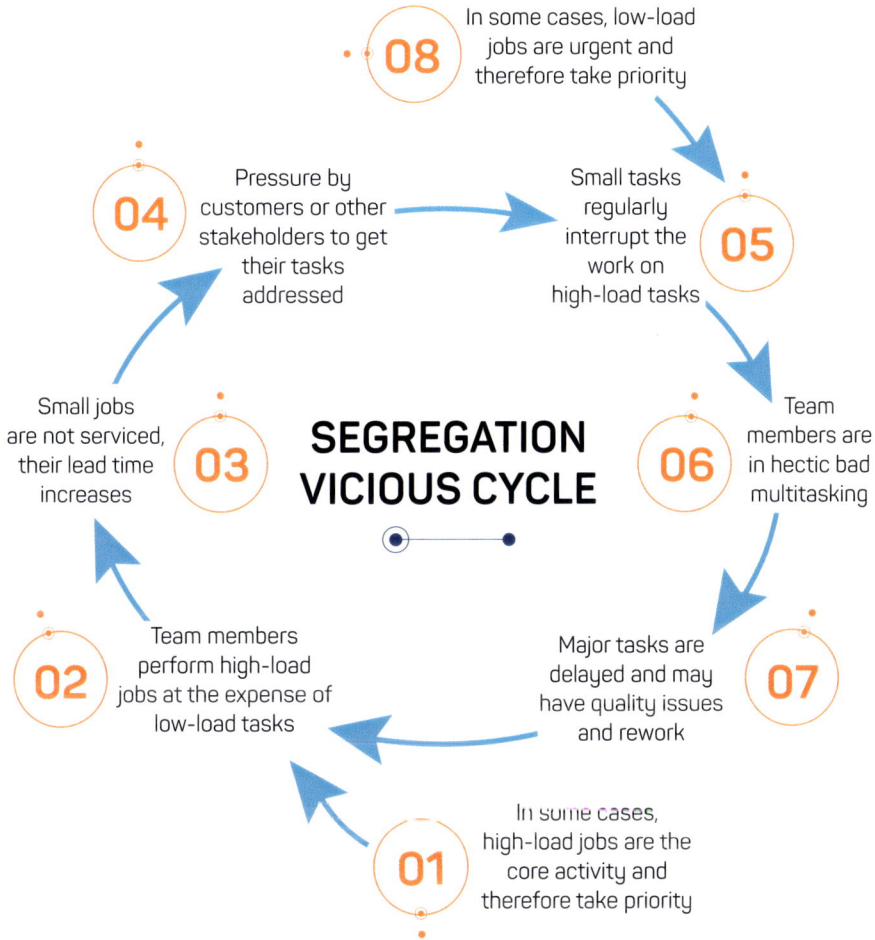

SEGREGATION VICIOUS CYCLE

08 In some cases, low-load jobs are urgent and therefore take priority

04 Pressure by customers or other stakeholders to get their tasks addressed

05 Small tasks regularly interrupt the work on high-load tasks

03 Small jobs are not serviced, their lead time increases

06 Team members are in hectic bad multitasking

02 Team members perform high-load jobs at the expense of low-load tasks

07 Major tasks are delayed and may have quality issues and rework

01 In some cases, high-load jobs are the core activity and therefore take priority

THE SOLUTION

To break the vicious cycle, the prevailing mix of low-load and high-load jobs must be challenged. The current approach brings team members to react based on the urgency of the job (low-load or high-load) rather than improving the flow and preventing the important jobs from becoming urgent. The primary objective should be to improve the flow with a "focus and finish" approach for small tasks and "don't multitask" approach on big jobs.

In order to establish a "focus and finish" environment, there is a need to segregate the work in a manner that decouples the interaction between low-load and high-load jobs. There are two ways to segregate work:

OPTION 1 | SEGREGATION BY RESOURCES

Strive to have high-load and low-load jobs executed by different team members. This way, low-load jobs would not be waiting for a high-load job to be completed, while high-load jobs would not be regularly interrupted by small tasks jobs. Team members' assignment does not have to be permanent. The important thing is not to assign low-load jobs to workers who are currently engaged in delivering high-load jobs. In case there are recurring issues with a specific team member, such as long waiting times for small tasks or delays in delivering large tasks, we should re-examine the task allocation to better utilize the capacity of this team member.

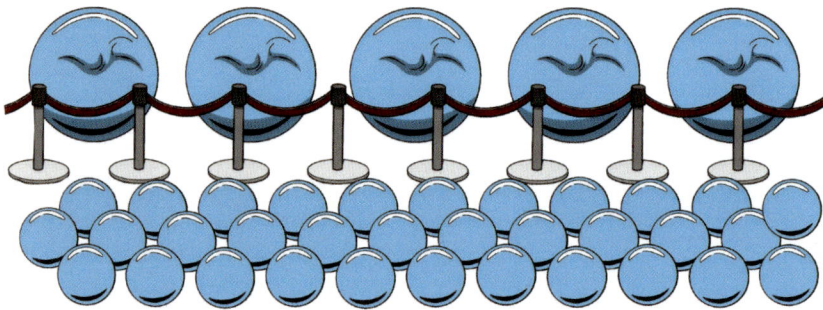

At the electrical equipment manufacturing company, regular engineering cabinet jobs were assigned to engineers who were available and not currently engaged in highly customized projects. This segregation approach assumes that workers possess the skills required to handle both low-load and high-load jobs, providing the flexibility to assign tasks based on worker availability. Such flexibility can also be utilized to have different workers handle rework as it arrives, based on availability, rather than on being strictly assigned to the worker who initially performed the task.

The accounting department recruited and assigned new team members specifically to handle routine ongoing tasks, allowing the more experienced staff to have the capacity to focus on high-load, complex projects. This division of labor leveraged the experience of seasoned employees for more demanding projects.

OPTION 2 | SEGREGATION BY TIME

Allocate a specific time slot to conduct either low-load or high-load type of jobs. For example, certain hours each day are reserved exclusively for high-load projects that require undisturbed focus, with all interruptions strictly prohibited during this time. Alternatively, separate slots can be assigned for low-load tasks, allowing the rest of the day to be dedicated to concentrated work on complex projects. Key to this approach is setting clear expectations among all stakeholders to respect the designated times and avoid disruptions. Meanwhile, workers are expected to fully utilize these slots, either wrapping up low-load tasks or making significant progress on high-load jobs. This alignment ensures effective time management and enhances productivity across the department.

In the hospital setting, a solution was implemented to segregate tasks by time to ensure that admitted patients received the utmost attention and care. This strategy was put into practice as follows:

● **Predefined patient care hours.** During these hours, doctors were solely focused on attending to their patients without interruptions.

● **Gatekeeper ward manager.** To prevent interruptions and ensure that urgent matters were still addressed promptly, the ward manager was assigned as the gatekeeper during the designated patient care hours. The gatekeeper was responsible for determining the urgency of inquiries from other wards, admitting only the urgent ones. With the gatekeeper ward manager in place, the medical staff could concentrate on its patients without frequent distractions. All hospital staff, including administrators, doctors, and support personnel, were briefed on the new time-segregation approach.

● **Handling inquiries in the backlog.** Non-urgent inquiries were dealt with throughout the day outside the segregated hours for dedicated patient care.

In the realm of software development, the company decided to implement the segregation-by-time approach to optimize their workflow, specifically when it came to code reviews versus code development. This was done by establishing the following:

● **Predefined time slots.** All relevant team members committed to being available for code reviews at dedicated timeslots. This way, code reviews were not delayed due to scheduling considerations. Anyone who needed a code review could ask for it on short notice, thereby speeding up the execution of the code review task without interfering with the core activity of code development.

● **No interference policy.** During designated code-development time slots, mainly in the morning, team members were instructed not to interrupt one another with unrelated tasks or questions. This allowed engineers to concentrate fully on developing and refining code without distractions. In the afternoons, the focus shifted to code reviews.

● **Stakeholder alignment.** To make this approach effective, the company ensured that all stakeholders, including managers, project leads, and team members were on the same page regarding the allocated time slots. Clear communication was essential to prevent any interference between high-load and low-load tasks.

● **A "Focus and Finish" mindset.** During code review time slots, engineers were committed to completing their reviews promptly, ensuring that feedback and improvements were delivered in a timely manner.

The development team, multitasking between high-load feature development and low-load bug-fixing, adopted a similar time-based segregation approach. This approach involved the following strategies to streamline workflow and ensure better task management:

● **Batching bug fixes and user interface updates into projects.** The team planned a release that would be focused on completing as many bug fixes and user interface updates as possible. This ensured that these tasks were completed in a segregated time window and did not interfere with high-load feature development.

● **Approval for interference.** Urgent bug fixes and user interface updates were allowed to intervene in the core development work, but only with prior approval from a high-level senior executive who served as a gatekeeper. This senior executive had a global view of project priorities and implications. Any proposed interference was recorded, and its potential impact on core development work was thoroughly analyzed before approval was granted. Regular evaluations were conducted to assess whether the approved interruptions were indeed necessary and if there were ways to minimize them in the future.

MANAGE BUFFERS | PROTECTING THE SEGREGATION APPROACH

In order to maintain the segregation solution, it is useful to establish time buffers and resource buffers.

● **Time buffer**. A time buffer is a pool of extra time to fulfill commitments. Implementing a Service Level Agreement (SLA) that aligns expectations on delivery times can be beneficial. Setting expectations for delivering low-load tasks creates a standard that can allow sufficient buffer time for focusing on high-load tasks. Note that the mix of low-load and high-load jobs can vary over time. On occasion, the delivery time expectation committed in the SLA is too aggressive and can lead to bad multitasking. If this is the case, consider increasing the committed service timeline defined in the SLA. If prolonging the lead time is not possible and the backlog of low-load tasks keeps growing, this calls for an increase of capacity.

● **Resource buffer.** A resource buffer is a reservoir of resources, in this case, worker capacity, which can be tapped in situations where the SLA is at risk of violation. Typically, these workers should be available on short notice so that they can join the low-load team to augment capacity and clear the growing backlog of low-load tasks. This resource buffer will be efficient only if at least some of the team members can perform both the low-load tasks as well as the high-load tasks. One way to build this buffer is to prioritize the assignment of tasks so that the less flexible people are assigned first, reserving the flexibility of more skilled workers for handling any surge in low-load tasks. In order to build this buffer, the assignment of tasks needs to be centralized.

While the above solution addresses the need for segregation of work, several obstacles may need to be addressed to.

HOW TO CAUSE THE CHANGE?

● **RESOURCE ALLOCATION CHALLENGES.** In many cases, due to their experience, the same workers are needed for handling both low-load and high-load jobs, which creates challenges when attempting to segregate work by resource. In such situations, the initial step is to challenge the assumption that the same people must handle both task types. Keep in mind that even though assigning these tasks to other people may reduce efficiency, the overall advantages in terms of workflow improvement can outweigh any such inefficiencies. If your tasks must be managed by the same workers, consider segregating them by time.

● **PRESSURE TO ADDRESS LOW-LOAD JOBS.** One common obstacle to implementing the segregation approach is the pressure to address low-load jobs promptly and prevent them from piling up in the backlog. In such cases, it's essential to first assess the process for managing tasks' execution. Are the tasks adequately organized and equipped for efficient execution (full-kit)? Are the tasks executed with the work dosage that enables "focus and finish?" It is crucial to remember that failing to complete these tasks within the allocated time will contribute to backlog growth. If the pressure to handle low-load tasks remains high, it may also be necessary to review the SLA or evaluate the overall capacity so as to manage these tasks effectively.

● **RESISTANCE TO CHANGE FROM TEAM MEMBERS.** When implementing work segregation by resources (workers), some team members may hesitate to let go of certain types of tasks. In such situations, it is important to communicate the overall benefits of the work segregation strategy. Highlight the personal challenges and difficulties that these workers currently encounter and emphasize how segregating tasks can address their pain effectively. Personalizing the benefits can help in gaining cooperation and buy-in from the team members involved.

● **INFORMAL COMMUNICATION CHANNELS.** The presence of informal channels of communication can breach the established segregation. These informal channels might involve friends requesting favors or hierarchical chains of command interfering with the new process. It is essential to actively identify and block these unauthorized lines of communication. Failure to do so can result in occasional interferences that, over time, may gradually erode the segregated work environment, eventually restoring the vicious cycle.

In some instances, it is useful to highlight noncompliance with the segregation policy. For instance, at an aerospace engineering company, specific hours were designated each day to allow engineers to work on their tasks without interruptions. If a manager violated this arrangement by requesting engineers to work on something else, that manager was required to contribute one dollar to the "doughnut jar." At the end of the week, the accumulated funds were used to purchase doughnuts for the entire department.

GUIDING QUESTIONS FOR GROUP DISCUSSION & IMPLEMENTATION

Follow these guiding questions to facilitate a discussion with your team on segregating tasks in your operation:

IDENTIFYING AREAS FOR TASK SEGREGATION

1 Is there a growing backlog of low-load tasks and/or hectic bad multitasking on high load tasks?

2 Do low-load jobs escalate into a crisis?

3 Do high-load jobs suffer from significant delays and quality issues?

SETTING UP FOR TASK SEGREGATION

4 In your environment, which is more feasible, resource segregation or time segregation?

5 How can we systemize the process of task allocation to workers to ensure proper resource segregation?

6 What challenges arise when trying to segregate work by resource, and how can we overcome them?

7 Is time-based segregation more feasible and beneficial? Which time slot should be allocated to low-load or high-load tasks? How do we create a "focus and finish" environment?

SUSTAINING THE RESULTS

8 What should be the SLA timelines for servicing low-load tasks? When considering segregation deployment, is there adequate capacity to meet the SLA?

9 How can we ensure that all stakeholders understand the rationale and advantages of task segregation and comply with it?

05
CHAPTER

ENSURE FULL-KIT

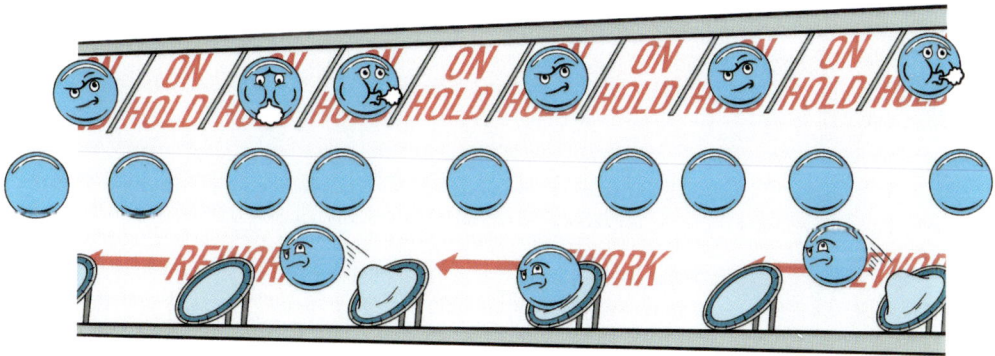

OBSTACLE TO FLOW

Too often, projects, or projects phases, come to a halt or require rework, because they were launched without all the necessary elements required for adequately completing the job. The requisite elements for a successful execution of a job (e.g., materials, resources, information, authorizations, etc.) are referred to as full-kit.

EXAMPLES

Software development: Initiating the coding phase of a software development project before having a well-defined set of requirements can lead to code rewrites, project delays, and increased development costs.

Marketing campaign launch: Launching a marketing campaign without finalized creative assets or a comprehensive marketing strategy can result in disjointed messaging, poor campaign performance, and the need for costly last-minute revisions.

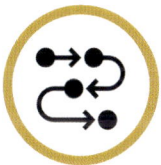

New product manufacturing: Starting the production of a new product before all necessary manufacturing processes have been thoroughly tested and optimized can lead to defects, production line stoppages, and increased quality control expenses.

Aircraft engine overhaul: In the aviation industry, performing an overhaul or major repair of an aircraft engine starts with disassembly and inspection, followed by a repair phase, and finally, assembly and testing. The integration of all parts at assembly can become a major challenge with delays in the repair process or in the procurement of replacement parts. Starting without all necessary replacement and repair parts, tools, and technical documentation leads to rework and delays in the assembly and testing process. Recovering from these delays results in rushing to procure missing parts or tools on short notice, which can be more expensive, both in terms of purchasing costs and expedited shipping fees.

Construction projects: Starting a phase in a construction project without all the required materials, tools, information, authorizations and without ensuring resource availability often leads to desynchronization among the different trades (e.g., electricity, plumbing, woodwork, flooring etc.). This results in delays, rework, work stoppages, budget overruns, and client dissatisfaction.

THE CHALLENGE

The pressure to make progress often compels teams to commence projects, project phases, or even tasks before all necessary requirements are in place. In some cases, there is a rush to hand off work to the next phase, even before it is fully completed. People trust that whatever is missing can be supplied as the work progresses. In certain scenarios, this practice becomes a primary source of significant delays, rework, and hectic multitasking in project execution.

One such scenario occurs when there are critical integration points within the project flow, where multiple inputs, such as materials, paperwork, designs, and workstream deliverables, must come together seamlessly to complete the next phase of the project. Launching the next phase without full-kit leads to frequent "start and stop" of workflow as something essential is found missing, causing delays and requiring exhaustive, often costly, expediting efforts. Another scenario in which proceeding without adequate preparations can be detrimental is when critical information is essential for accurate task execution. If workers have to start working before this information arrives, they will have to make assumptions about the missing information. And if it turns out that they guessed wrong, they will have to start all over again.

In the above scenarios, it is highly beneficial to implement a full-kit practice, establishing gates in the project flow where work cannot advance to the next phase without having all the requirements in place to complete the phase once it is set in motion.

INDICATORS

How can we tell if starting without full-kit prevails in our environment? Determine if the following indicators are common issues faced by the team:

● **LACK OF CLARITY ON REQUIREMENTS:** There is a lack of clarity regarding the requirements needed to complete a job. Work can start with incomplete information but often needs rework as better information is provided.

● **FREQUENT START AND STOP SCENARIOS:** Team members frequently commence a job only to have to stop, waiting for something essential. During these interruptions, they often switch to other tasks.

● **HIGH WORK IN PROCESS:** There is a high level of WIP that sits idle because of missing or pending elements such as materials, authorization, information, or resources.

● **OVERLOADED KEY RESOURCES:** Key resources (experts and/or expediters), essential to keep work flowing, are often greatly overloaded. They engage in frantic multitasking across projects, with priorities characterized as "red, red hot, and drop everything and do it now."

● **FREQUENT NEED FOR REWORK AND ITERATIONS:** Getting the work done without carefully aligning it with the correct specifications leads to frequent rework and iterations. These issues are frequently discovered in later phases of the project.

● **LATE SURPRISES:** Missing information or requirements are discovered late in the project, leading to significant delays when there is not enough time left to recover.

THE VICIOUS CYCLE

Review the vicious cycle with your team to ensure alignment on the core challenge. Many inputs (such as materials, information, authorization, workstream deliverables, etc.) are needed to make adequate progress in the project, but often these inputs are not readily available (1). When this happen, since there is pressure to complete the work on time (2), and we often believe it will take too long to assemble the full-kit (3), work will often start without all the requirements in place (4). Now, although we trust that missing items will arrive on time, too often it is merely wishful thinking. Hence, work on projects often comes to a halt since something critical is missing or because it is not carried out to specification (5). The numerous start and stop scenarios and rework delay the project completion far beyond the planned due date (6). Now, there will be mounting pressure on key experts to rectify the situation, expedite the work, and to hand off the work to the next phase even before the current phase is fully completed (7). In consequence, these experts will not be available to full-kit, intensifying the practice of starting work without all requirements in place (4), thereby perpetuating and worsening the vicious cycle.

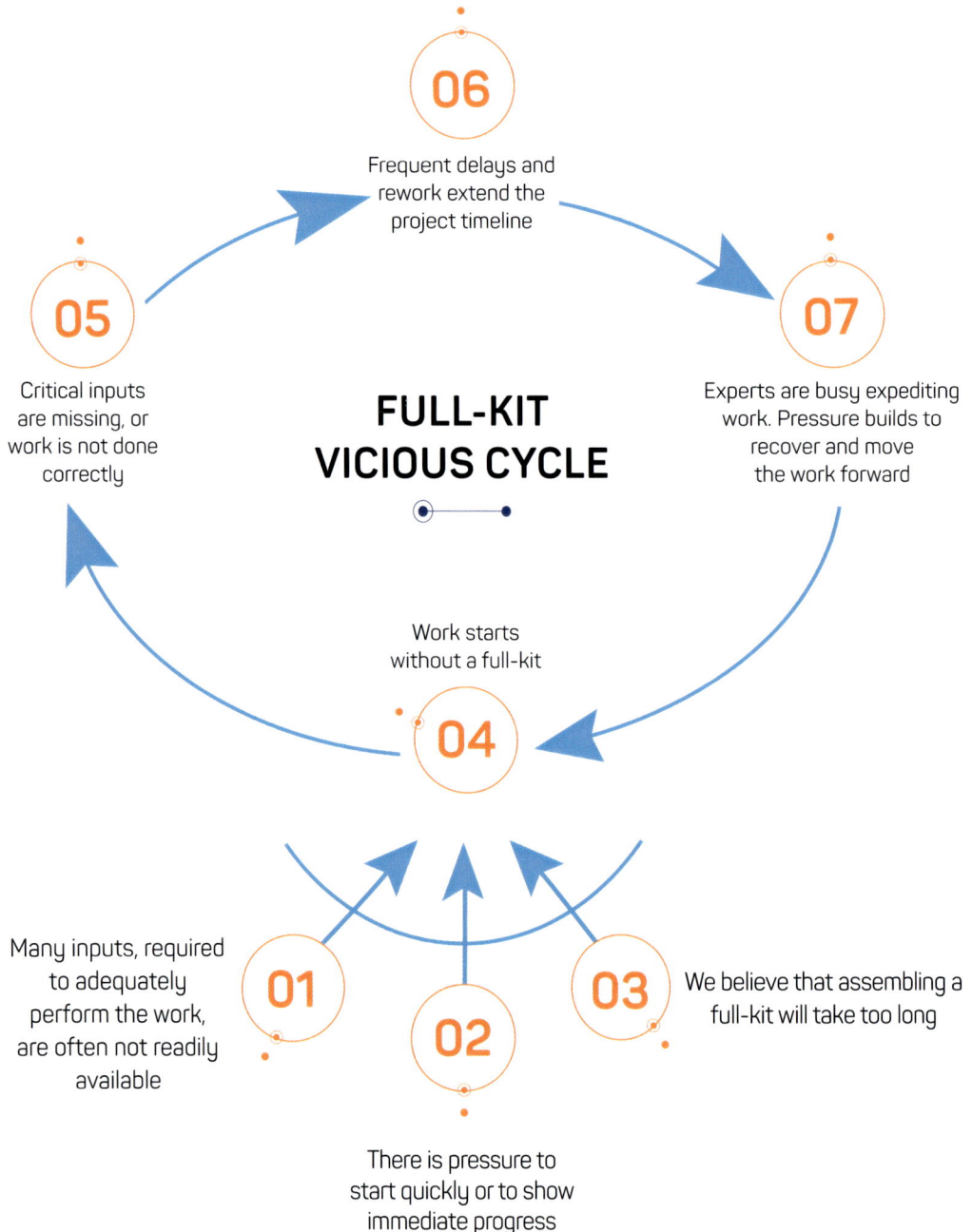

06

Frequent delays and rework extend the project timeline

05

Critical inputs are missing, or work is not done correctly

07

Experts are busy expediting work. Pressure builds to recover and move the work forward

FULL-KIT VICIOUS CYCLE

Work starts without a full-kit

04

Many inputs, required to adequately perform the work, are often not readily available

01

02

03

We believe that assembling a full-kit will take too long

There is pressure to start quickly or to show immediate progress

THE SOLUTION

The current practice of showing progress motivates starting the work before all necessary requirements are ready and, in particular, incentivizes rushing to start work on the next project phase prematurely. This results in frequent "start and stop" events, prolonging cycle times and causing rework. The focus should not be on how soon work starts but on how fast work is completed. The remedy lies in establishing a system that ensures, in the majority of cases, the timely availability of full-kits and a discipline that enforces the rule that work is allowed to start only when all inputs essential to complete it are available.

To systematically establish a full-kit practice, the following steps should be implemented:

STEP 1 | **MAP CRITICAL PHASES IN THE PROJECT.** Define the phases of work that need to be executed without having to stop in the middle due to missing inputs. This can be the entire project, a stage of the project, or even a task in the project.

STEP 2 | **ASSIGN A FULL-KIT ENFORCEMENT MANAGER**. The full-kit enforcement manager plays a crucial role in ensuring the timely availability of full-kits for the appropriate tasks and phases of the project. This role can be assumed by the project manager or by a function responsible for managing certain tasks across different projects. Typically, the full-kit manager needs to be a person with authority to stop work on the project if the requisite full-kit is not ready.

STEP 3 | **IDENTIFY ENFORCEABLE GATES**. Define the gates within the project flow where the full-kit rule must be rigorously enforced. These gates typically correspond to the following cases:

- Project integration points.
- Project phases where work transitions from one resource or department to another.
- Project phases where work is being done by less experienced workers who need guidance by experts.
- Onset of major project phases, where the absence of crucial information would likely result in rework.
- Launch of projects, where typically there should be a gate ensuring a full-kit before the project starts execution.

STEP 4 | **SPECIFY THE FULL-KIT REQUIREMENTS FOR EACH GATE**. This list should be curated by experienced workers who have a deep understanding of what is necessary to maintain smooth workflows. The full-kit should not aim to be an exhaustive list encompassing all possible requirements (trying to do so might result in excuses not to start the work). Instead, it should include all requirements necessary to ensure smooth progress. Note that the personnel needed to define, create, and determine full-kits typically consists of experienced experts in the field. When we assign them to specific tasks, we consume their capacity. Their critical capacity should be managed and should be utilized as much as possible for the full-kit role.

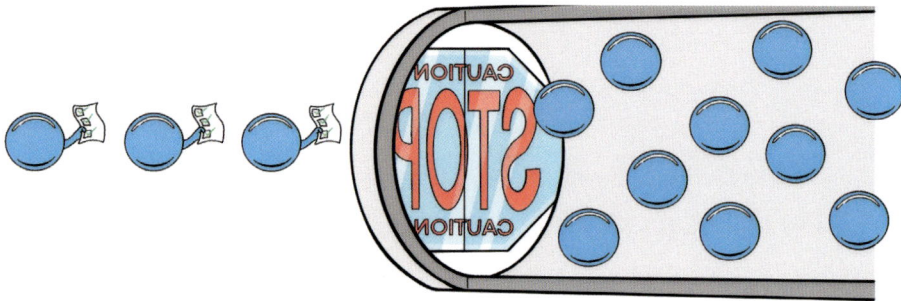

Here are a couple of examples of project gates and corresponding full-kit lists. In each of these examples, generic full-kits were defined, and multiple gates were established at the beginning of critical phases. When preparing full-kits for each project, the generic lists are customized to the specific requirements of the project at hand:

SOFTWARE DEVELOPMENT PROJECT

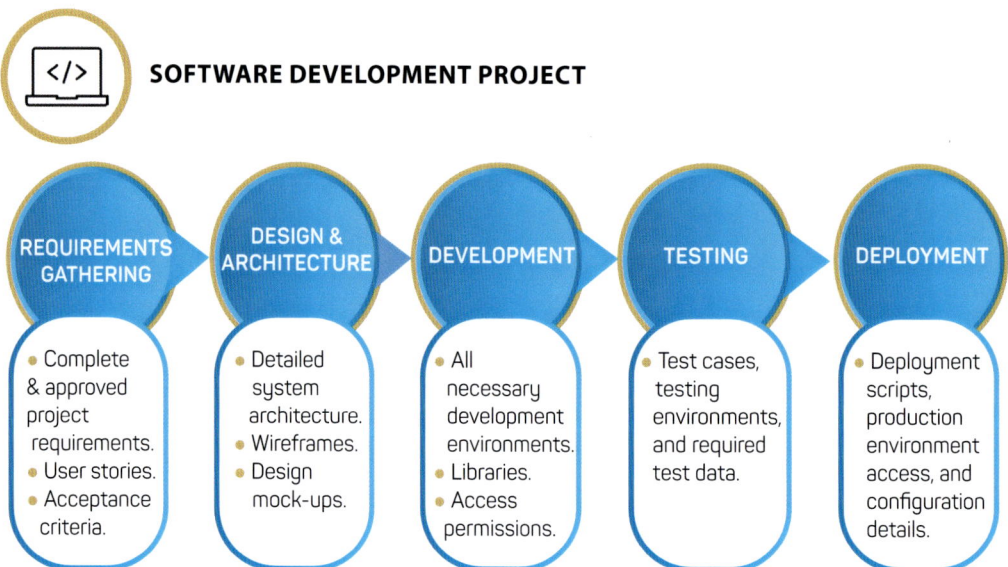

REQUIREMENTS GATHERING	DESIGN & ARCHITECTURE	DEVELOPMENT	TESTING	DEPLOYMENT
• Complete & approved project requirements. • User stories. • Acceptance criteria.	• Detailed system architecture. • Wireframes. • Design mock-ups.	• All necessary development environments. • Libraries. • Access permissions.	• Test cases, testing environments, and required test data.	• Deployment scripts, production environment access, and configuration details.

CONSTRUCTION PROJECT

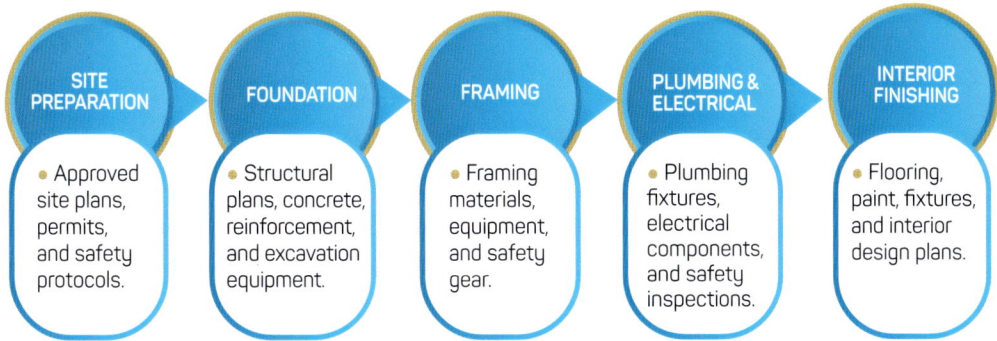

SITE PREPARATION	FOUNDATION	FRAMING	PLUMBING & ELECTRICAL	INTERIOR FINISHING
• Approved site plans, permits, and safety protocols.	• Structural plans, concrete, reinforcement, and excavation equipment.	• Framing materials, equipment, and safety gear.	• Plumbing fixtures, electrical components, and safety inspections.	• Flooring, paint, fixtures, and interior design plans.

STEP 5 | **ESTABLISH A FULL-KIT MANAGEMENT PROCESS**. Develop a process to ensure full-kit readiness in a timely manner. This process should guide the full-kit manager in monitoring kit assembly and completion, and in raising alerts if there is a risk of not completing the full-kits on time.

STEP 6 | **ENSURE THAT THE PROJECT HAS A BUFFER TO ABSORB ANY DELAYS IN COMPLETING THE FULL-KIT**. In order to ensure adherence to the full-kit discipline, it is necessary to have a sufficient time buffer. The buffer will ensure that there is enough time to ready the full-kit, thereby reducing the pressure to start without a complete full-kit in case of full-kit assembly delays. See Chapter 9 on how to create time buffers.

STEP 7 | **MONITOR FULL-KIT COMPLIANCE**. Implement a measurement system to monitor compliance, ensuring that kits are consistently ready on time and identifying instances where work begins without a full-kit on hand. To refine the flow continuously, do the following:

Track and analyze instances when full-kits fall short of completion within the allocated time frame. Examine what elements were missing and determine if there is a recurring pattern or common cause behind full-kit incompleteness.

Track instances when a project phase is delayed despite having a ready full-kit. Such analysis will reveal if we are missing a requirement for the full-kit.

Track job delays and their underlying reasons to help strengthen the full-kit requirements for the phase.

FULL-KIT PROCESS	Map critical phases in the project **01**	Assign a full-kit manager **02**	Identify enforceable gates **03**
Specify the full-kit requirements for each gate **04**	Establish a full-kit management process **05**	Incorporate buffers to absorb delays in completing the full-kit **06**	Monitor full-kit compliance **07**

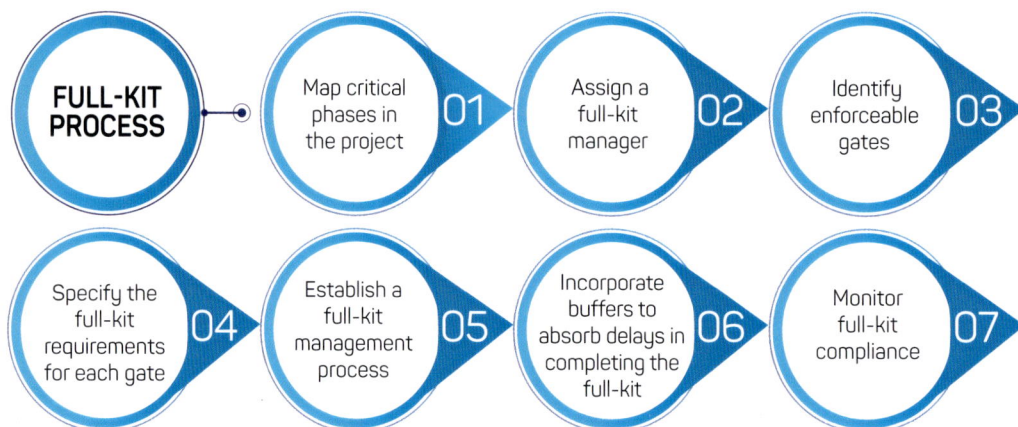

HOW TO CAUSE THE CHANGE?

Implementing a full-kit practice will likely raise a concern that waiting for the kit to be completed will significantly delay the start of work. To address this concern, it is crucial to ensure that the organization is devoting enough time, resources, and management attention to ensuring full-kits.

To initiate the process, it is essential to engage appropriate top leadership in the full-kit monitoring process. Often, this can be accomplished by putting an executive in charge of the full-kit process and setting a regular meeting with an agenda focused on reviewing all full-kits and initiating problem-solving efforts to resolve outstanding problems.

Implementing full-kitting often goes hand in hand with efforts to reduce WIP for improved efficiency. Projects currently in WIP, but without a ready full-kit, are identified and moved to a backlog list, pausing them to free up capacity. This newly available capacity can then be used to speed up projects that are fully kitted, as well as to prepare full-kits for backlog projects. Although challenging to implement, this approach significantly boosts full-kit quality and speeds up project execution throughout the pipeline.

Another practice to avoid delays is to notify, in advance, the workers responsible for full-kitting about upcoming projects, allowing them sufficient time to prepare. These alerts can be triggered at various time milestones before the start date, a process known as 'T minus preparation'.

GUIDING QUESTIONS FOR GROUP DISCUSSION & IMPLEMENTATION

Follow these guiding questions to facilitate a discussion with your team on applying the full-kit discipline in your operation:

THE NEED FOR THE FULL-KIT DISCIPLINE

1 Which projects in execution are missing ready full-kits? How many projects have a ready full-kit?

2 In which areas does work often wait for missing full-kit elements?

3 In which areas could rework have been prevented with a ready full-kit?

4 Which managers or experts multitask the most and have to resolve execution problems stemming from incomplete kits?

5 How relevant are the list of indicators and the vicious cycle?

SETTING UP TO FULL-KIT

6 Where in the project flow should we establish full-kit gates?

7 Who should define the full-kit? What should be in it?

8 How can we free up capacity to prepare the full-kit?

9 Who should make sure the full-kit is ready on time?

SUSTAINING THE RESULTS

10 How should we monitor full-kit compliance?

11 How should we improve full-kit performance (full-kit in time)?

INCREASE WORK DOSAGE

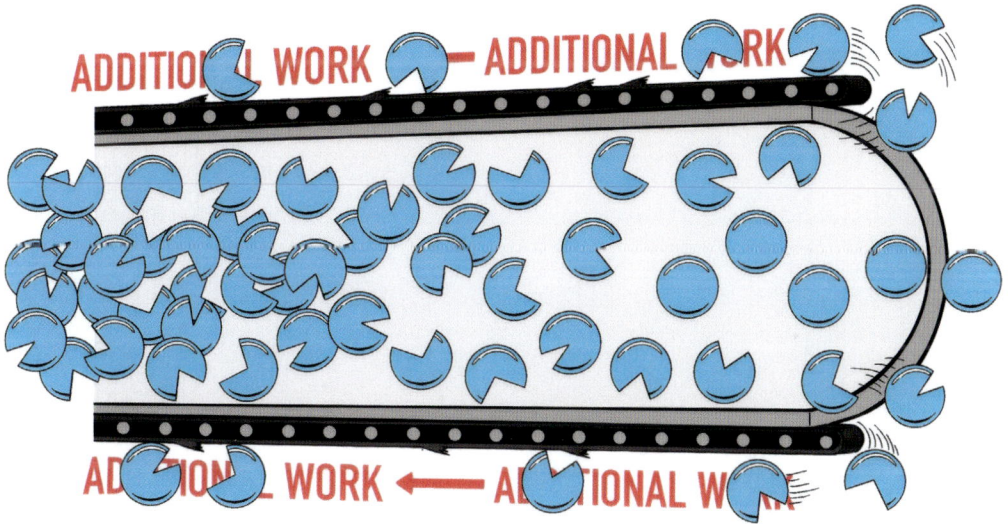

OBSTACLE TO FLOW

The pressure to address many tasks leads to allocating lower work dosage to each task, causing them to frequently return for more work dosage.

EXAMPLES

Social care personnel are tasked with assessing the eligibility of families in need of state support, but the volume of cases they handle can be overwhelming. As a result, they often try to meet with as many prospects as possible each month, allocating only a short time to each meeting. Prospects frequently need to schedule multiple appointments over several months to complete the entire process and provide all the necessary information to determine their eligibility.

Line maintenance teams carry out aircraft maintenance overnight at the airport. The need to maximize the availability of all aircraft compels them to focus only on essential fixes required for each aircraft to fly the next day. The work scope performed during overnight maintenance is limited to the minimal maintenance checks prescribed for a very short time horizon. In consequence, aircraft are returned to maintenance stations for further checks. This cycle can result in reduced asset availability and reduced network flexibility in routing aircraft, as each aircraft must return to a specific airport for maintenance.

Customer success representatives are tasked with ensuring that customers use products effectively and with identifying opportunities to upsell. Typically, they manage a lengthy list of accounts and are required to contact each customer periodically, according to a strict KPI specifying how many customers they need to message, email and call, and how frequently. Garnering adequate attention and cooperation from customers can be challenging. Consequently, representatives often move on to the next customer to meet their contact quotas instead of dedicating sufficient time and effort to make meaningful progress with the most promising accounts.

THE CHALLENGE

In certain environments, team members are constantly required to attend to a large number of tasks, but the backlog of tasks grows more rapidly than the available capacity. Faced with this overload, the team often finds itself compelled to prioritize quantity over quality, allocating only limited time and effort to each task before moving on to the next. Consequently, this approach compromises the team's ability to make significant progress on any given task. As a result, tasks frequently need to be revisited, thereby squandering valuable capacity. In such settings, contrary to the current practice, team members should dedicate more time and effort to each task when they are attending to it. By increasing the work scope's dosage, the team can either complete tasks outright or, at a minimum, significantly increase the period before tasks require attention again.

INDICATORS

How can we tell if there is a need to increase a work dosage in our environment? Determine if the following indicators are common issues faced by the team:

● **HIGH WIP WHICH IS CONTINUOUSLY INCREASING**. Examples include the number of cases per social care worker, the number of assigned customers per customer success representative, and the volume of open maintenance work on aircraft.

● **A MEASUREMENT INCENTIVIZING A HIGH VOLUME OF TASK HANDLING WITHIN A GIVEN TIME INTERVAL.** Such measurements tend to focus on quantity with a minimal requirement of scope.

● **A MINIMAL STANDARD OF DEFINED WORK IS MANDATED.** The defined work is often much lower than what could be accomplished. For example, maintenance personnel perform the minimal tasks required to prepare the aircraft for flight the next day. Social services provide the minimal level of support mandated by law.

● **EACH TASK REQUIRES MULTIPLE ITERATIONS TO MAKE PROGRESS.** Airplanes frequently undergo line maintenance, with a series of inspections and repairs. In social services, meetings with prospects occur multiple times until eligibility for support is determined. Customer success representatives maintain frequent communication with customers' personnel until tangible results are achieved.

THE VICIOUS CYCLE

Review the vicious cycle with your team to ensure alignment on the core challenge. The number of tasks required to be performed significantly exceeds the available resources' capacity (1). As a result, the tasks' backlog increases. More tasks are added to the task queue, and waiting times lengthen (2). In order not to keep tasks waiting for too long, and perform them faster, the organization puts in place metrics and incentives to perform as many tasks as possible within a set timeframe (3). To keep up with their measures, resources now provide a low work dosage to each task (4). Low work dosages frequently loop tasks back for additional work (5). In turn, this increases the backlog of tasks even further (2).

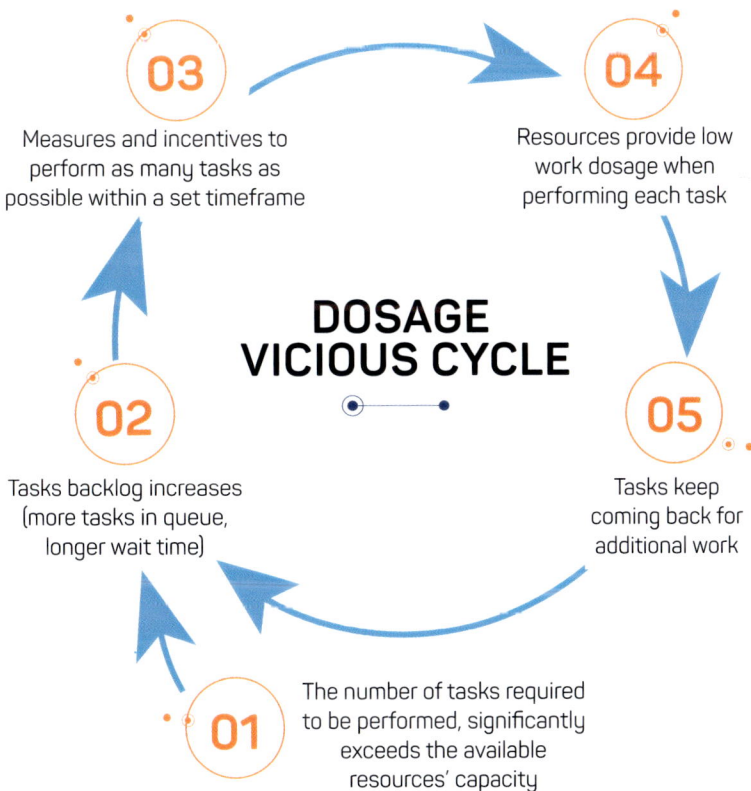

03
Measures and incentives to perform as many tasks as possible within a set timeframe

04
Resources provide low work dosage when performing each task

DOSAGE VICIOUS CYCLE

02
Tasks backlog increases (more tasks in queue, longer wait time)

05
Tasks keep coming back for additional work

01
The number of tasks required to be performed, significantly exceeds the available resources' capacity

THE SOLUTION

The current practice of low work dosage prevents us from making much progress with each task. We keep looping back to the same tasks for further work, eventually increasing the backlog and, with it, the turnaround time. To break this vicious cycle, we should increase the dosage so that significantly fewer tasks loop back for further work and tasks are completed faster than new ones are added to the backlog.

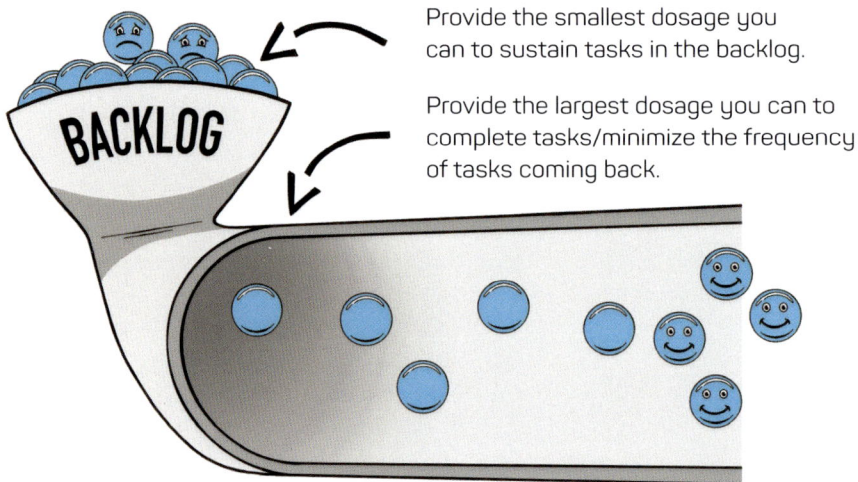

Provide the smallest dosage you can to sustain tasks in the backlog.

Provide the largest dosage you can to complete tasks/minimize the frequency of tasks coming back.

The process to determine and provide a higher work dosage is as follows:

STEP 1 | **DEFINE THROUGHPUT METRICS AND PROGRESS MILESTONES.** We must define throughput metrics that clearly indicate when a task is complete (e.g., either because we managed to get it out of the system or because we gained a long window of time until it needs to come back for more work). The scope of the task should be clearly defined in terms of the progress milestones that need to be reached in order to get the task completed.

STEP 2 | **REDUCE THE CURRENT LEVEL OF WIP AND INCREASE THE WORK DOSAGE PROVIDED TO EACH ACTIVE TASK.** The goal is to increase the dosage sufficiently to minimize the frequency of tasks looping back, ensuring that the rate of incoming tasks is less than the rate of tasks completed. It is essential to increase the dosage to create a buffer, resulting in substantially more throughput (as defined in step 1). This approach allows us to maintain a high dosage even during temporary disruptions that increase the backlog. Without this buffer, we face pressure to release tasks from the backlog by reducing the work dosage, which could lead us back into a vicious cycle.

STEP 3 | REMOVE CONTRADICTORY METRICS. Identify and revise metrics that incentivize quantity over quality and counter the increase of work dosage.

STEP 4 | PROVIDE SOME SERVICE WORK TO BACKLOGGED TASKS. While tasks wait in the backlog queue, pressure keeps building to attend to them. Providing a limited-service work to the queued tasks will ease the pressure to release them into the WIP. Not doing so will force us back to providing low work dosage, and the vicious cycle will reappear.

STEP 5 | CONTINUE TO REDUCE WIP AND INCREASE WORK DOSAGE. Determining what is the right level of WIP and work dosage is a gradual process. We should start with an increase in dosage that improves results, and then continue to increase it as long as it is feasible and results in additional throughput.

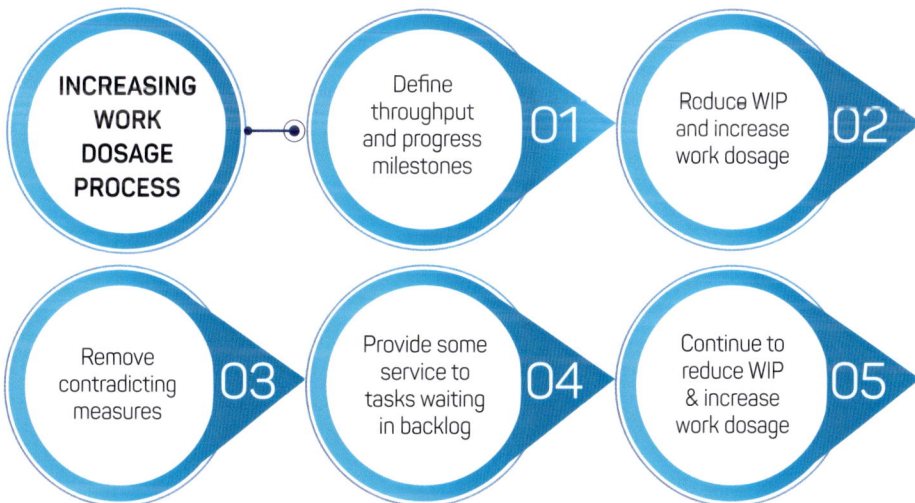

INCREASING WORK DOSAGE PROCESS

Define throughput and progress milestones **01**

Reduce WIP and increase work dosage **02**

Remove contradicting measures **03**

Provide some service to tasks waiting in backlog **04**

Continue to reduce WIP & increase work dosage **05**

Let us consider some examples of applying the above steps:

AIRCRAFT LINE MAINTENANCE

Defining throughput and progress milestones. Throughput is defined here as flight hours available until the aircraft needs further maintenance. Often, this metric is termed the "health" of the aircraft. Increasing the health increases the airline's flexibility in flying the aircraft throughout its network. This increased flexibility creates operational buffers that improve on-time performance and often translate into higher asset utilization and higher revenues. Generating health requires that a group of checks and fixes needs to be accumulated into a work batch. The completion of each work batch is a progress milestone.

● **Reducing WIP and increasing work dosage.** Maintenance work dosage should be adjusted to ensure that the health period generated every day through maintenance exceeds the health period consumed. Note that each day the aircraft does not undergo maintenance, the health period of that aircraft is reduced by one day. An aircraft that undergoes maintenance gains a health period commensurate with the maintenance dosage provided. For example, assume a fleet of 100 aircraft. How many aircraft should undergo maintenance each day, and what work dosage should be assigned to each aircraft? In practice, we wish to cut the WIP to the extent that the health period generated each day exceeds the health period consumed that day. A simple approach is to cut the number of aircraft being maintained each day in half and check if that suffices to increase the throughput of health generated to stay ahead of health consumption. In this example, assume that currently, 20 out of 100 aircraft undergo maintenance every night, and each maintained aircraft generates 4 days of health for a total of 80 health days. Notice that the health consumed every day is 100, so the health deficit is 100-80=20 days. This situation leads to a vicious cycle. The first step is to cut the number of aircraft undergoing maintenance every day to 10 and aim to generate more than 10 days of health for every maintained aircraft, thereby generating more than 100 health days.

It is important to verify that the higher work dosage would generate more than 100 days of health. This would ensure a health buffer in case there are disruptions that prevent maintenance from generating the requisite health (100 days) on a particular day. Without such a buffer, the health throughput may drop below the incoming rate (=new maintenance needed). Typically, the buffer can be sized to provide sufficient time to recover from disruptions. In practice, monitoring the health of the fleet over a period of time will reveal if the buffer is too big or not big enough. The buffer also provides a mechanism to prioritize which aircraft should next be released into the WIP. The health of an aircraft will determine the priority for returning it to maintenance. Aircraft with the least health should have the highest priority.

● **Remove contradictory metrics**. In aircraft line maintenance, there is a defined maximal time interval to perform a check on a part. For example, a part may have to be inspected every week, or every month, or once every six months. In some cases, this interval may not be a fixed time interval but instead a function of the accumulated hours flown by the aircraft. For example, the interval may be a maximum of 200 hours of flying, or 500 hours of flying, etc. For checks to be efficient, the maintenance operation tries to minimize the number of times a check is performed in a year. For example, if a certain check must be performed at least once a month, maintenance will try to perform it only 12 times a year. This incentivizes performing maintenance as close as possible to its deadline. In order to increase the work dosage, this local efficiency metric must be subordinated to maximizing the health of the aircraft fleet as a whole. For example, if the target is to generate 30 days of health for each maintenance operation of the aircraft, then all checks due in the next 30 days need to be performed as a batch, even if this results in more checks per part per year. Under such an increase in work dosage, the improved maintenance throughput will more than compensate for the loss in efficiency.

● **Servicing the backlog.** The increase in maintenance work dosage reduced the aircraft's frequency of undergoing maintenance. This releases some capacity for maintaining the backlog of aircraft. Backlog aircraft are provided with only minimal maintenance which is absolutely necessary. Note that restricting the WIP of aircraft undergoing maintenance with high dosage is done gradually over a period of time, with incremental increases for as long as the generated health exceeds the health consumed. Such a gradual process ensures that the backlog of aircraft (which also requires some maintenance) is not inflated at once.

SOCIAL WELFARE

● **Defining throughput and progress milestones.** Throughput is measured here as the number of concluded cases where the family or person (customer) receives the state support to which they are eligible. The process of approving state support is composed of several milestones (e.g., obtaining needed information, verifying the information, evaluating options for support, etc.). Moving from one milestone to the next signals progress in the case until eligibility is determined.

- **Reducing WIP and increasing work dosage.** An increased work dosage helps speed up the progress from one milestone to another by increasing the quality and frequency of the interactions and reducing wasteful iterations with each case. Overall dosage should be increased to ensure that the rate of concluded cases outpaces the rate of incoming cases. How many cases should be handled per time period, and what should be the work dosage per case? The guidance here is to reduce the number of cases handled by a caseworker and increase the work dosage as cases are concluded faster. For example, a typical interaction of a caseworker with a customer involves meeting with the customer, gathering required information, recommending actions, and recording the interaction. Typically, such a meeting takes about an hour. A caseworker handling 60 cases at a time and spending 30 hours a week meeting case customers can only meet with a customer once every two weeks. The work dosage per case per week can be increased to two hours over a two-week period by cutting WIP to 30 cases. If it helps achieve progress faster, the work dosage can be increased to four hours every two weeks. The WIP will then consist of 15 cases.

As long as the case output rate is higher than the case input rate, the case backlog reduces. This provides a buffer to manage temporary peaks in new case arrivals or lost throughput due to delays, which temporarily increase the backlog. The way to monitor this buffer is by observing the waiting time of cases in the backlog. We can set a maximal wait time, such as one month, to be assigned to a caseworker. This buffer provides a "safety stock" of service time for managing temporary peaks in new case arrivals. If this buffer is too small, it means that the waiting time is set too short. Any delays in the treatment of active cases will increase backlog waiting beyond expectation. If the buffer is set too big, resulting in long waiting times, then people waiting to get help will get frustrated. In practice, the buffer can be sized by monitoring the backlog over a period of time to ensure that it is not too big or too small. The backlog waiting time should be set at a level acceptable to applicants waiting for help and enable us to manage the peaks in case arrivals. The buffer also provides a mechanism for prioritizing cases to be released into WIP. The case with the longest wait time should have the highest priority to be added to the WIP.

● **Remove contradictory metrics.** In welfare support, caseworkers are measured by the number of cases they handle. For example, when a caseworker is responsible for 60 cases at a time, they will be incentivized to meet with each case at the same time interval, thereby reducing the work dosage of each case and compromising outcomes. Instead of this metric, shifting focus to the number of cases concluded in a time period changes the incentives and encourages caseworkers to allocate the work dosage necessary to achieve meaningful progress.

● **Servicing the backlog.** While the open tasks (active cases) are being worked on with a higher work dosage, newly arrived cases should be serviced with the available capacity. Such service will aim to prep new cases for engagement before they turn "active." The social care agency conducted group meetings for newly arrived cases to educate them about the process, regulations, and needed information. Such service made sure that cases in the backlog were not feeling ignored and served as an initial full-kit to accelerate their progress when the cases were activated.

CUSTOMER SUCCESS REPRESENTATIVES

● **Defining throughput and progress milestones.** Increasing throughput would correspond to increasing product usage among customers, increasing conversion rates of low-usage customers to higher usage, and the identification and realization of upsell opportunities. The process to achieve higher throughput consists of reaching several milestones (e.g., reaching the right contact person, verifying the current usage status, establishing the need for further usage, getting agreement on the solution, etc.).

● **Reducing WIP and increasing work dosage.** An increased work dosage should aim to enhance customer engagement with a product, ensuring the customers derive tangible and meaningful benefits. The work dosage per customer is the number and quality of contacts made over a period of time that reach the milestones of each customer. Customers should be ranked based on their potential value to the business. Higher-value customers should receive a higher-dosage treatment. Note that a limit of minimum and maximum dosage must be set to determine when a task (customer) is considered complete, either because the next throughput milestone was attained or because efforts were exhausted, and we reached a point of diminishing return. The increased work dosage will require having a lower number of customers in WIP. For example, doubling the work dosage will reduce the WIP handled by the customer success representatives by half.

The increase in work dosage should provide higher throughput (successful customer engagement with the product). The work dosage should be increased to create a buffer of results beyond what we aim to achieve. This will reduce the pressure to spread attention thin with low work dosage. The buffer is monitored by observing the backlog. For each account, a maximal wait time can be set before the backlogged customer is contacted by a representative. This maximal time can be small for accounts of high value and higher for accounts of lower value. Monitoring the remaining buffer time of each account is used to determine the next account to be released into the WIP.

- **Remove contradictory metrics.** Customer success representatives are often measured by the number of customers contacted over a period of time and the time interval to contact each customer. The pressure to meet this metric may result in reducing the work dosage provided to selected customers. More informative metrics would include tracking the increase in product usage across customers, conversion rates of low-usage customers to higher usage, and the identification and realization of upsell opportunities. With these metrics, customer success representatives would increase the work dosage assigned to the right customers and in the right sequence in order to realize the desired outcomes.

- **Servicing the backlog.** Customers that are ranked low or are in the backlog for a while are serviced by a general customer success staff members who sample the customer's engagement and ensure they are not overlooked.

HOW TO CAUSE THE CHANGE?

Although the increase in work dosage would increase throughput, various stakeholders may not be inclined to collaborate.

- Management may be worried that, although we speed up tasks, the rate of completed tasks will go down.

- Operators may be concerned about not meeting their KPI targets, which incentivizes the quantity of tasks in WIP.

● Stakeholders may become alarmed if their tasks are waiting in a queue and work on them has not yet started. Their concerns are likely to escalate to higher levels, possibly reaching top management.

We should, of course, explain why increasing work dosage would eventually lead to higher throughput, reiterating that, after all, this is the overall objective. However, if ignored, the above concerns may still block the change. We should therefore introduce the change through a POC, that demonstrates that higher work dosage would lead to higher throughput. Nothing works like actual, tangible results.

Designing a POC involves careful planning and execution to test the effectiveness of increasing treatment dosage. Below is a step-by-step approach to designing a POC:

1 IDENTIFY A REPRESENTATIVE AREA. Select a small but representative area within the current process amenable to the implementation of an increased work dosage pilot. This area should be indicative of the broader system.

2 DEFINE SUCCESS CRITERIA. Clearly define the success criteria for the pilot. Determine the specific increase in throughput that will be considered successful.

3 IMPLEMENT INCREASED WORK DOSAGE. Apply the increased work dosage to the chosen representative area. Monitor and track the performance meticulously during this phase.

4 EVALUATE THE PILOT. Evaluate the results against the predefined success criteria. Determine if the increased work dosage led to the desired increase in throughput and if any other positive effects or learnings were observed.

5 DEFINE NEXT STEPS FOR EXPANSION. Based on the learnings, determine the feasibility and potential benefits of expanding the increased work dosage approach to the entire process or other relevant areas.

Remember, in order to ensure compliance with the POC, workers should not be subject to misguided metrics that incentivizes quantity over quality. Once the POC is successful, these metrics should be replaced by metrics that measure compliance to the new process and are focused on progress and throughput.

Another possible concern, of internal stakeholders, or external ones (e.g., customers), might be that their tasks are not being treated early enough. While increasing the work dosage for active tasks leads to faster completion overall, they worry that the tasks waiting in the backlog queue could create "noise." The pressure to treat these tasks will demand attention and reduce the work dosage assigned to active tasks, and the vicious cycle will reappear. To address this concern, one possible solution is to decouple the process by creating a dedicated step for handling new tasks. This step would focus on making the necessary preparations so that once the task is activated, there won't be any unnecessary delays. By implementing this approach, we can ensure that both active tasks and new tasks receive appropriate attention and timely treatment. Another possible solution is to provide backlogged tasks with updates on their activation time. Over time, the reliability of these updates will assuage concerns about backlogged tasks and reduce pressures for their early treatment.

GUIDING QUESTIONS FOR GROUP DISCUSSION & IMPLEMENTATION

Follow the guiding questions below to facilitate a discussion with your team on ensuring proper work dosage in your operation:

IDENTIFYING AREAS FOR REEVALUATING WORK DOSAGE

1   Which area experiences the dominant pressure to prefer quantity over quality, involving many tasks, as opposed to going deeper into each task?

2   Do jobs require multiple iterations until they are completed? Do they often come back for further work?

3   How relevant are the list of indicators and the vicious cycle?

SETTING UP TO INCREASE WORK DOSAGE

4   What is the throughput (in terms of goal units per unit of time) of the entire process? How do we measure the generation of more goal units?

5   What should be the reduced WIP level (open jobs worked on) to enable a substantial work dosage increase?

6 What additional work dosage should be given per task to reduce iterations and increase throughput?

7 How do we service the backlogged tasks waiting to enter the process?

SUSTAINING THE RESULTS

8 Do we have enough buffer to sustain disruptions?

9 Who may be concerned with reducing WIP and increasing work dosage? How to address their concerns?

10 How to measure success?

STANDARDIZE
TO SCALE

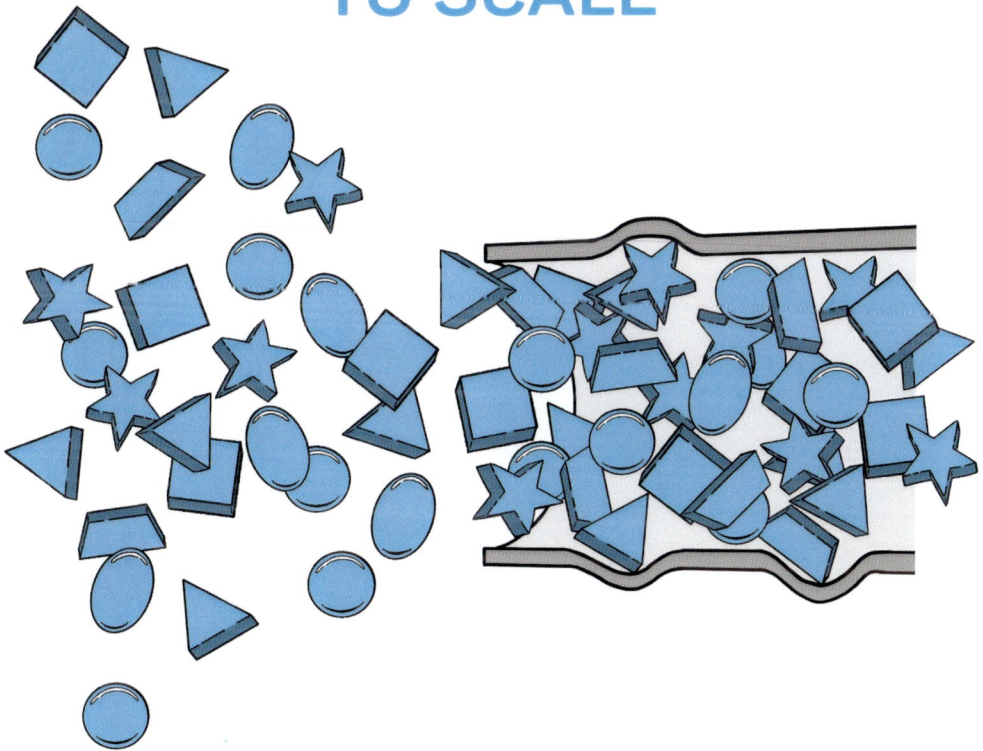

OBSTACLE TO FLOW

Work carried out by less experienced workers often falls short, necessitates rework, and poses challenges to scaling without compromising quality standards.

EXAMPLES

An aerospace company has successfully developed a prototype that showcases the potential and value of a product it intends to introduce into the market. However, the transition from prototype to meeting market demand involves complex engineering and design requirements. To expedite time-to-market, the company quickly expands its engineering team. A significant challenge arises because the initial prototype lacks comprehensive documentation; it contains a wealth of tacit knowledge held by the experts who were part of its initial design. As new engineers join the team, they find themselves trapped in cycles of rework due to the absence of critical information. Simultaneously, the experts are firefighting to resolve issues while building the necessary capacity to adhere to the product's schedule, which is slipping.

A machinery manufacturing company made a strategic decision to expand by entering new market segments, resulting in a surge of orders requiring engineering solutions and designs vastly different from their existing products. This influx of new engineering work has left senior engineers overwhelmed as they grapple with these challenges while simultaneously managing their existing workload. Less experienced and newly hired engineers who were tasked to support the traditional business suddenly found themselves without much guidance. Rework mounted, adding additional load on the veteran engineers.

A fintech startup has created a microservices app for personal finance management, seamlessly integrating it with the legacy IT systems of several banks. This app provided an exceptional experience for bank account holders and earned the trust of the banks, leading to its expansion. With secured funding, the startup aimed to scale by onboarding new banks and adding modules and features to the app. To achieve the aggressive growth targets, they brought in additional developers. However, the increased workload of creating product interfaces that could integrate with the legacy systems of new banks, combined with the pressure to meet the product development roadmap, placed a substantial burden on the development team. As a result, the core development team found themselves stretched thin, juggling between addressing emerging issues, training newcomers, and meeting the growth milestones committed to investors.

A founder-owned boutique digital marketing agency, known for its creative and tailored campaigns, is receiving a surge of client requests due to its growing reputation. The founder decides to hire more team members to handle the increased workload. New team members, though talented, aren't immediately attuned to the unique creative approach and quality standards that have defined the agency. The founder finds himself stretched, balancing client work, overseeing and correcting the team's outputs, and trying to instill his creative ethos.

THE CHALLENGE

In certain environments, such as R&D, engineered-to-order, startups, or service-oriented organizations, work is often diverse and nonstandard. As these organizations scale, or when they battle high staff turnover, their experts face a surge of nonstandard work. Less experienced workers struggle without sufficient guidance, leading to rework and waste. The experts become overwhelmed with rectifying work, training others, and managing their tasks. Workers yearn for clear guidance, but the urgency of tasks prompts them to start without waiting for expert advice. Simply calling for Standard Operating Procedures (SOPs) is ineffective, as the experts needed to develop them are already overburdened. A practical solution must first enhance the utilization of experts, followed by creating and institutionalizing SOPs, training, and compliance mechanisms.

INDICATORS

How can we tell if low standardization and high reliance on experts is a prevailing obstacle in our environment? Determine if the following indicators are common issues faced by the team:

● **HIGHLY DIVERSE WORK.** Work is highly customized, with significant freedom in execution leading to varied approaches. Lacking standard processes, even the same type of work can be performed differently by the team.

● **VARIABLE LOAD AND LEAD TIME.** There is a noticeable variability in workload and lead times. The unpredictable workflow and varied approaches to doing the work make it difficult to estimate timelines, and planning becomes a daunting task.

● **INCREASED REWORK AND ITERATIONS.** Less experienced workers, trying to navigate non-standardized processes, inevitably make errors causing a great deal of rework and iterations.

● **OVERBURDENED CRITICAL EXPERTS.** Skilled professionals are swamped, torn between rectifying errors, dedicating time to their primary tasks, and coaching and helping team members. The success of the business increasingly relies on the availability of these key experts, thereby creating a high degree of risk.

● **INTENSIVE WORK MONITORING.** As delays and mistakes multiply, there is a constant need for close monitoring of work, and status meetings proliferate. This adds an additional burden on experts.

● **CHALLENGES IN RAMPING UP THE TEAM.** Developing the capabilities of new team members to make them productive can be quite challenging. Team members find themselves in a predicament where they simultaneously complain about the lack of clear guidelines while also having to adhere to guidelines that aren't particularly relevant to the specific tasks they are working on.

THE VICIOUS CYCLE

Review the vicious cycle with your team to ensure alignment on the core challenge. Work in this environment is highly diverse and, at times, undertaken for the first time (1). It goes without saying that to perform such work at high standards, experienced, skilled experts are required, and they are not easily found. Now, likely for valid reasons, the organization is rapidly scaling up or taking on a significantly higher workload (2). Inevitably, the experts become overloaded and struggle to perform all their responsibilities efficiently (3). The pressure to get things done while the experts are overloaded leads to handing tasks to less experienced people. Since the work is not standard, and clear guidelines to cover all possible scenarios are not available, these workers often perform the tasks inadequately (4). Consequently, there is a high level of rework, delays, waste, and dissatisfied customers (5). The experts are called to rectify the work and coach and help others, all this while performing their daily tasks (6). In addition, the high level of rework, delays, and overall dissatisfaction adds pressure to standardize processes. Much of this pressure comes from less experienced workers who get stressed and yearn for clear procedures. This pressure to standardize work, which is highly diverse and customized, often leads to imposing procedures prematurely (7). Since the procedures cannot cover all scenarios, there will be many exceptions and workarounds, often resulting in additional mistakes. The burden on experts will increase even further, requiring them to fix mistakes and continuously revise SOPs (6). In consequence, the capacity of the experts is drained even further (3), and the pressure to hand the work to less experienced team members grows further.

Notice, the same vicious cycle applies when rather than rapidly scaling (2) the organization experiences high staff turnover.

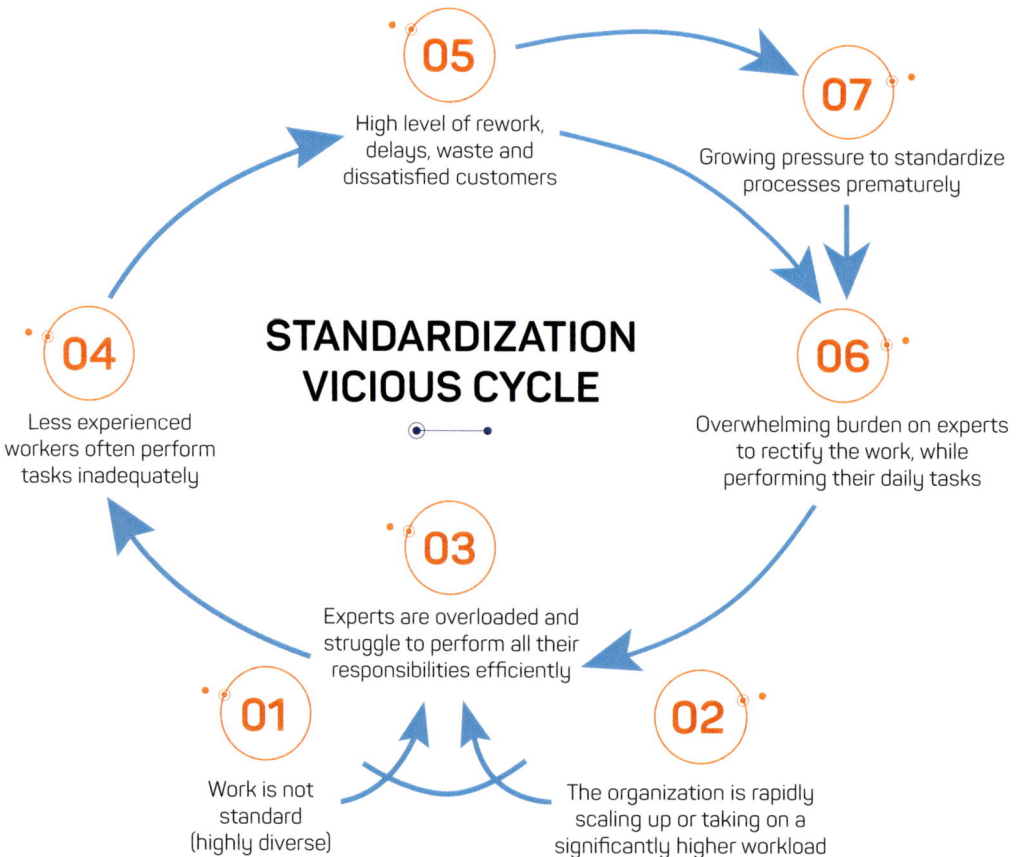

STANDARDIZATION VICIOUS CYCLE

05 High level of rework, delays, waste and dissatisfied customers

07 Growing pressure to standardize processes prematurely

04 Less experienced workers often perform tasks inadequately

06 Overwhelming burden on experts to rectify the work, while performing their daily tasks

03 Experts are overloaded and struggle to perform all their responsibilities efficiently

01 Work is not standard (highly diverse)

02 The organization is rapidly scaling up or taking on a significantly higher workload

THE SOLUTION

In environments that depend on experts (the constraints), when the organization scales, managers attempt to support the growth by replicating current practices and adding more and more resources. However, the primary focus should be on improving flow to accommodate the much higher level of nonstandard work. Accordingly, we should leverage the experts' capacity in a very different manner. The key is to focus the experts' capacity on the critical jobs that only they should do while ensuring that others perform their tasks productively and systematically. Standardizing the work means that it can be done with low experts' involvement. Freeing up experts' capacity to allow them to prepare and monitor less experienced members to carry out their work, is in fact part of the standardization effort. Overall, it reduces the involvement of experts in carrying out the work itself. Over time, work could be further standardized (reduce experts' involvement) by creating SOPs and mechanisms that steer people to perform the work in a systematic manner, guided by the SOPs.

The process to leverage the experts' capacity in a manner that standardizes the work and successfully scales the operations, includes the following steps:

1 | **IDENTIFY THE EXPERTS' CRITICAL WORK.** Understand which work is difficult to standardize and, therefore, should continue to be done by certain experts.

2 | **REMOVE NON-EXPERT WORK FROM THE EXPERTS.** Relieve the experts as much as possible from duties that are unrelated to their core job.

3 | **LEVERAGE EXPERTS TO STANDARDIZE THE WORK AND SUPPORT SCALE.** Ensure that work done by the non-experts is full-kitted by experts and minimize experts' direct involvement in the actual tasks.

4 | **SCALE IN A WAY THAT KEEPS THE LOAD ON THE EXPERTS MANAGEABLE.** Realign the offering portfolio and go-to-market activity in a way that reduces the impact on experts.

5 | **DEVELOP MORE WORKERS TO PERFORM AT EXPERT LEVELS.** Build an on-the-job expert skill development system.

6 | **ENSURE SUFFICIENT CAPACITY BUFFERS.** Align hiring and development targets to prevent the experts from being overloaded.

Let us elaborate on the above steps:

STEP 1 | IDENTIFY THE EXPERTS' CRITICAL WORK

Locate the stages in the process where rework is prevalent. Typically, this will be work that requires the judgment of experienced experts who are overburdened and suffer from hectic, bad multitasking. Define this critical work that needs to be done with high quality. Determine which experts, if engaged early enough, could eliminate or reduce rework.

For example, the **aerospace company's team** that built the prototype has significant tacit knowledge that is undocumented. This team has the expertise to resolve the technical challenges created by conflicting product requirements. Their role in scaling the prototype to a market-ready product is to ensure that the conflicting requirements are resolved consistently with the prototype concept. If this role is delegated to others, the impact will be felt in terms of increased iterations of design cycles.

STEP 2 | REMOVE NON-EXPERT WORK FROM THE EXPERTS

Often, the experts perform jobs that are peripheral to their expertise. These are often jobs they carry over from previous roles or jobs they were given due to their managerial position, such as HR and other administrative duties. Try to free up the experts' time to focus on work within their scope of expertise while ensuring they have the responsibility and authority to do so. While it is important for the experts to have authority to ensure that their judgment is respected, it is essential to minimize experts' time spent on administrative and management tasks. Otherwise, such tasks will consume much of their precious capacity.

STEP 3 | LEVERAGE EXPERTS TO STANDARDIZE THE WORK AND SUPPORT SCALING

● Ensure the work being done by the non-experts is full-kitted by experts. Now that we have freed up some of the experts' capacity, it can be utilized to prepare non-experts to perform non-standard work. It will enable to accommodate a much higher workload while maintaining high standards. Additionally, it will further increase the experts' capacity, as less time will be spent fixing the high volume of mistakes made by non-experts. Essentially, the expert's job should be to full-kit the work at "gate zero" —before it is commenced. Full-kit, in this context, means making all decisions that require expert judgment and defining the step-by-step process for non-experts to carry out the work. Full-kitting the work by experts involves developing a protocol for executing the tasks. Essentially, the experts' role is to standardize the process, enabling others to carry it out independently without needing direct expert involvement. This approach helps mitigate the risk of mistakes and iterations. To fully leverage this step, it is important to ensure full-kit compliance. Delay the start of a job until experts have fully kitted the work, ensuring that all necessary resources and information are available to proceed efficiently. Implement gates beyond which work cannot progress without the explicit approval of an expert, ensuring that the next phase is sufficiently standardized.

● Since judgment is always involved in task execution, when experts provide comprehensive instructions to less experienced workers, it is essential to highlight situations where the worker should make independent judgments, and where they should seek expert guidance. As part of this guidance, experts should not only explain "what to do" but also "why to do it." Articulating the reasoning behind each step, (e.g., why a particular action is taken, why one action is chosen over another, and why a specific step is performed before another), serves to reduce dependence on experts. It empowers nonexperts to make follow-up decisions without constant expert involvement, thereby restricting the need for guidance only to cases where the underlying reasoning changes.

● Monitor the compliance with full-kit process. Identify cases where less experienced individuals handle tasks without sufficient preparation by an expert. This situation signals a process breakdown, possibly due to insufficient expert capacity (ensure that all tasks not requiring expert skills have been delegated).

● Minimize experts' direct involvement in the actual task execution. Look for hidden capacity in the experts' routine. Some experts prefer to spend the time doing the job themselves. This may be due to inertia since this is what they used to do before they became experts, or because they are tired of rework. Review the experts' routine and look for additional jobs that can be carried out by others if provided with a full-kit. The experts' actual involvement should be limited to tasks that require their expert judgment. Reserve experts' capacity to full-kitting and solving problems that happen despite full-kitting.

● In the process of full-kitting the work, experts should typically also develop templates, automation tools, decision trees, and standardized forms that limit options for non-experts, thereby reducing their opportunity to make mistakes.

In **the aerospace company** case, experts performed stress analysis to size the airframe structures. These experts can either do the work themselves or help full-kit the work in order to allow less experienced engineers to become productive. As the full-kit process matures, these experts can document their decision-making process, including guidance on which analysis to do, ranging from hand calculations to full finite-element models, what margins to use, what analysis guidelines to follow, and how to write the analysis reports for regulatory compliance. They can also be actively involved in working with the structural design team to solve problems by modifying the design. These activities would leverage their expertise rather than letting them actually perform the actual analysis work.

In **the fintech startup**, the experienced developers know how to integrate with the legacy systems of existing bank customers. This knowledge would make them the natural choice to do this work for the new banks. While the development and testing of these interfaces was a lot of work, the real expertise was in understanding the interface requirements and developing the mapping between the company's data requirements and the way this data was captured in the legacy systems. Experienced developers working to develop and test the interfaces would constitute a constraint. A better approach is to use these experienced developers to full-kit the work for the less experienced developers by creating specification documents. Over time, as the full-kit process matures, the expert knowledge can be incorporated into a standard process, supported by automation tools for developing the interfaces. Non-experts can then perform the simpler task of using such automation tools to develop the interfaces. This kind of work that codifies the knowledge of the experts would more effectively leverage the experienced developer's capacity toward supporting the company's growth.

STEP 4 | **SCALE IN A WAY THAT KEEPS THE LOAD ON THE EXPERTS MANAGEABLE**

Evaluate markets and offerings based on the impact on the experts' capacity as compared with their value to the business. Challenge the assumption that to get more sales, it is necessary to expand offerings and portfolio complexity. Remember that the result of portfolio rationalization should be a far more reliable and faster service of higher quality. Such careful choices of markets and offerings can build "healthy" growth of the business.

For example, **in the fintech startup**, rapidly onboarding banks with different legacy systems will overwhelm the developers' capacity. By focusing on banks with similar legacy systems, the fintech startup can accelerate the adoption of its product while minimizing operational risks. Such a focused approach will help build the tools, standards, and business partnerships that maximize value for the startup and minimize the impact on the experts.

The machinery manufacturing company faced the challenge of handling an increasing volume of orders requiring engineering solutions and designs vastly different from their existing products. To reduce this complexity, sales efforts were directed only to certain segments, where the core design of machines was common, and customizations were mainly concerned with interfaces and dimensions.

Kitchen Nightmares is a reality TV series in which renowned chef Gordon Ramsay is invited by owners to help revive their struggling restaurants over a week. Each episode begins with Chef Ramsay being shocked by the restaurant's delayed service and poor quality of the courses, leading to unhappy customers and frequent disputes among the restaurant staff. A consistent solution, implemented by Chef Ramsay in his turnaround strategy and featured in nearly every episode, is simplifying the menu to consist of fewer options. His philosophy emphasizes concentrating on a limited number of dishes, ensuring that they are served promptly, and maintaining high quality.

STEP 5 | DEVELOP MORE PEOPLE TO PERFORM AT EXPERTS' LEVEL

● Pair experts with apprentices to facilitate knowledge transfer and skill development. For example, when apprentices help the experts prepare the full-kits in early project stages, both the apprentice and expert benefit. Apprentices gain a deeper understanding of the projects, and when possible, they take some of the load off the experts. On-the-job training is key to the development of new workers in a non-standard work environment.

● Establish clear criteria for evaluating people's expertise and competence. Ensure that the pathways to higher competence are clearly mapped out.

● Specialize workers by repeatedly engaging them in the same kind of work to accelerate their growth in capability and expertise. With increasing expertise, these workers will become more independent of the experts.

In the case of **the boutique digital marketing agency**, the owner divided roles among the team based on their ability to perform in various stages of the marketing campaign creation. These stages were Campaign Planning (strategy development and market research), Content Creation (creatives and design), and Project Management (campaign execution, monitoring, and optimization). The approach of using an "all-around player" for expert-level performance in all tasks was found to be unsuitable for growth. Instead, specialized roles were defined for each phase, allowing team members to quickly gain expertise and handle these tasks effectively at scale. More experienced experts took on the role of mentors for new recruits, guiding their development. The initial stages of the marketing campaign, particularly the Campaign Planning stage, required more judgment and an intimate understanding of the founder's creative style. Recognizing this, the founder, who once managed all aspects of the agency, now focuses primarily on Campaign Planning alongside the most skilled team members. This focus ensured high quality and creative excellence. For the Content Creation and Project Management stages, where the founder's direct input was less critical, standardized protocols were established. This approach freed up the founder's capacity to monitor all stages from a broader perspective, ensuring that the work adhered to the creative vision that set the agency apart.

● Monitor how you help people grow their capabilities and expertise and attempt to identify bottlenecks in the development process. The bottlenecks can be in the selection of expert candidates, in the training process (e.g., are they empowered? are they pushed to develop capabilities?), in applying the training feedback, in filtering out wrong candidates, etc. These bottlenecks should be addressed to accelerate growth. Progress can be measured by monitoring the number of apprentices at different levels of expertise and the time it takes these apprentices to improve their capabilities.

STEP 6 | ENSURE SUFFICIENT CAPACITY BUFFERS

● Scaling requires the company to have sufficient workers at expert levels. Hiring targets that are not aligned with the demand placed on experts' capacity results in pressure to delegate non fully-kitted work to less experienced workers, thereby risking the emergence of a vicious cycle. It is beneficial for the HR department to maintain a continual buffer of expert candidates.

● Shortages of non-experts' capacity can pressure experts to perform tasks that others should do. It is important to ensure adequate protective capacity of non-expert resources.

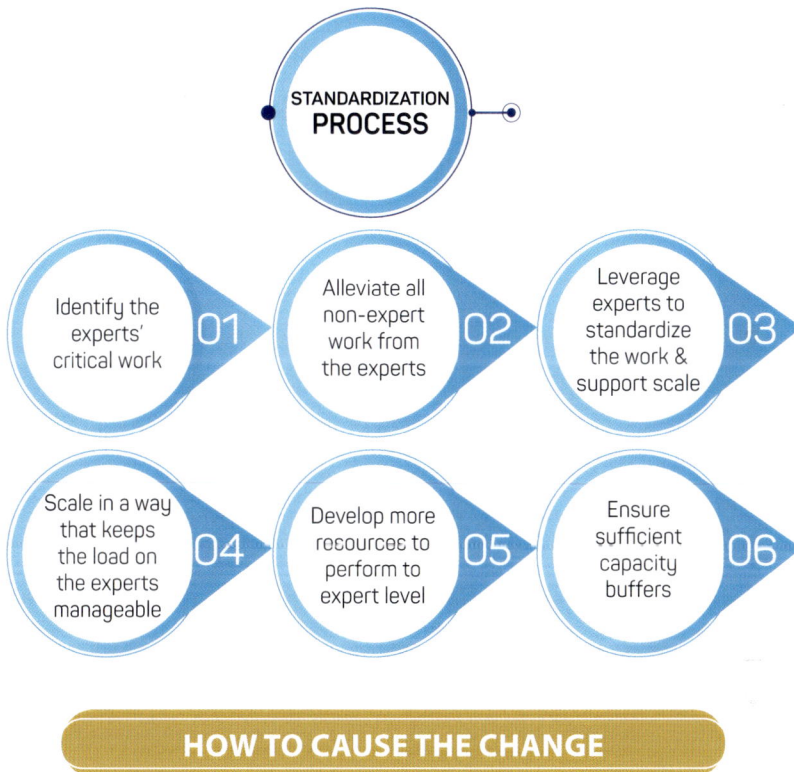

STANDARDIZATION PROCESS

01 Identify the experts' critical work

02 Alleviate all non-expert work from the experts

03 Leverage experts to standardize the work & support scale

04 Scale in a way that keeps the load on the experts manageable

05 Develop more resources to perform to expert level

06 Ensure sufficient capacity buffers

HOW TO CAUSE THE CHANGE

Several obstacles might need to be overcome to effectively apply the standardization solution:

● **EXPERT AVAILABILITY.** As mentioned, one common challenge is that experts are often engrossed in actively doing the work in current projects, leaving them with little or no time to full-kit upcoming projects. To mitigate this problem, it is essential to limit the tasks that experts perform in current projects and limit the projects that are in progress (WIP), thereby ensuring that experts have sufficient capacity for full-kitting work. Note that in order to implement this stage, the organization must allocate the time and expertise to process mapping, defining the gates for experts' intervention, and the full-kit definition for each gate.

● **ROLE ACCEPTANCE.** Experts might resist adopting a new, more horizontal role that demands less direct involvement in specific projects. This reluctance could stem from personal preference and also doubts about the less experienced staff's ability to execute tasks effectively. Addressing this concern involves emphasizing the benefits of the reduced rework and errors resulting from early expert involvement. It may also be necessary to incentivize the change by conferring higher decision-making authority for the experts.

● **BUSINESS PRIORITIES.** A significant hurdle may arise if pausing major market initiatives is necessary to free expert capacity. The company needs to quantify the benefits of focusing on fewer initiatives in terms of speed, scaling, and avoiding costly mistakes.

● **SALES FOCUS.** The sales department, accustomed to diversification, might find it challenging to concentrate on selling to more focused customer segments. To instill this focus, a realignment of their performance metrics and incentives might be required to reinforce the shift towards standardization.

GUIDING QUESTIONS FOR GROUP DISCUSSION & IMPLEMENTATION

Follow the guiding questions below to facilitate a discussion with your team on reducing dependency on experts and increasing work standardization in your environment:

IDENTIFYING THE RELIANCE LEVEL ON EXPERTS

1 Where is expert judgment needed to ensure high quality and avoid mistakes?

2 Where is rework most prevalent, and which experts possess the skills and knowledge to mitigate it?

3 How relevant are the lists of indicators and the vicious cycle?

LEVERAGING EXPERTS IN SCALING

4 How can we free experts' capacity? What administrative and management tasks are the experts involved in?

5 At what stages should experts be engaged to ensure full-kitting of non-standard work?

6 Which market segments and offerings generate high value for the requisite expert capacity?

DEVELOPING CAPABILITIES FOR SCALING

7 Which stages of work can be further standardized by establishing SOPs?
Who should create them? How do we ensure compliance?

8 What are the pathways for less experienced workers to gain capability and expertise?

9 What is the rate of progress these workers make along these pathways?

CHAPTER 08

SYNCHRONIZE RESOURCES & ACTIVITIES

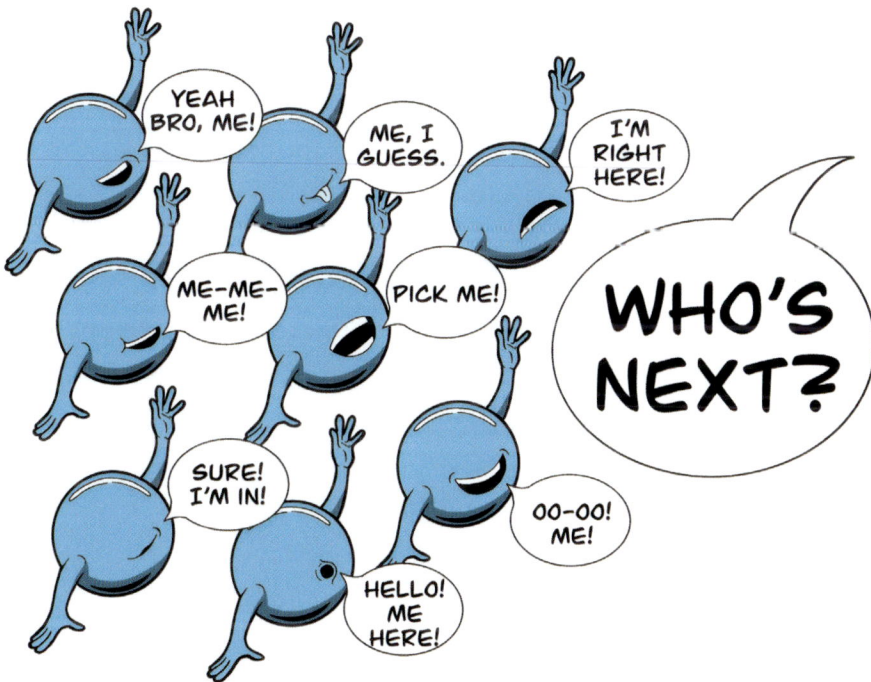

OBSTACLE TO FLOW

Team members prioritize tasks based on local considerations, which are often not aligned with global priorities, thereby causing delays that are typically discovered in latter stages of the project.

EXAMPLES

Construction of a multi-storied residential tower. In a construction project, multiple teams work in parallel, each carrying out their trade, such as electrical, plumbing, controls, finishing, painting, etc. The trade teams are eager to be more productive and make progress with their job. There is some degree of flexibility in the sequence of work, which allows each trade to work at its own pace. Under pressure to make progress on the volume of work (e.g., amount of wiring completed, amount of piping laid, number of equipment and appliances installed, etc.), the trades work on any work front available. In the short run, this leads to progress for each team but ultimately results in dramatic slowdowns as finishing becomes difficult with trades team members multitasking across the different work fronts. In addition, quality problems, resulting from trades work not performed in synch, lead to rework and iterations, which considerably delay completion times.

Engineering complex equipment like aircrafts and ships. A typical project in such an environment involves the integration of design activity across teams working on systems (e.g., electrical, mechanical, propulsion, etc.) with teams working on structures. In a complex engineering project, progress at the project level is determined by the rate at which technical risks are resolved. Often, different teams work at their own pace based on their local priorities. The result is that integration risks are revealed late in the project and often require costly iterations. For example, when working on a certain aircraft, the structures team was able to advance at a faster pace and complete the design of the structure much earlier than the teams working on systems. Consequently, the systems teams were forced to fit the systems into a predefined structure, leading to compromises in functionality. This situation eventually required iterations for both the systems and the structures, causing major delays to the project.

Assembly of complex equipment. This is a multi-project environment, where each piece of equipment delivery is a separate project. Often, these environments are plagued by missing sub-assemblies and parts. Many project assemblies proceed concurrently, but each of them may be missing sub-assemblies or parts. As the orders for the complex equipment are delayed, there is pressure to "cannibalize" parts from one order to complete another. This leads to a chain of rework and iterations as parts are constantly transferred from one piece of equipment to another.

THE CHALLENGE

Workers often carry out tasks according to their own convenience or efficiency priorities, unaware that they end up hindering the timely completion of the overall project. The attendant misalignment of priorities grows as the workload increases. Team members have more open tasks to choose from, increasing the likelihood that they will not select the right tasks. Furthermore, there is a growing pressure on each member to use local considerations in order to improve productivity. These misalignments result in considerable wait times at integration points where the work of various teams needs to come together to make progress. This is where we typically discover the implications of working guided by local priorities.

Misalignment in priorities can also result in significant mistakes and rework when teams are performing tasks concurrently on a certain project, each at its own pace. Often, to make progress, teams that work at a faster pace decide not to wait but rather make assumptions regarding the work of other teams and start the work. This behavior inevitably results in mistakes that call for rework, typically revealed at the latter stages of the project, when the work of the various teams needs to be integrated.

To synchronize work, a clear and uniform prioritization mechanism is required. Such a mechanism should continually guide each team member to prioritize the tasks in a manner that best supports the timely completion of overall projects.

INDICATORS

How can we tell if there is a need to improve synchronization in our environment? Assess if the following indicators are common issues faced by the team:

● **TEAM MEMBERS HAVE FLEXIBILITY TO DEVIATE FROM THE SUGGESTED PLAN**. Often these deviations are considered to be minor. However, when many teams deviate from the suggested plan, the result is considerable desynchronization in the latter stages of the project.

● **HIGH VOLUME OF TASKS.** Teams have to work on many tasks which can be worked on in any order. The high volume of work puts pressure to sequence the work based on local efficiency considerations. This is often the case with shared resources performing tasks across work streams.

● **CONSIDERABLE WAITING TIMES FOR INTEGRATION.** Work proceeds rapidly at first, but there are integration problems and rework cycles as the work progresses, and the work of multiple teams needs to be integrated.

● **LATE DISCOVERY OF TECHNICAL PROBLEMS.** Technical problems that cause major redesign efforts and delays are discovered late in the project. Many of these problems could have been avoided with proper synchronization across the various teams working on the project.

● **PROJECT PLANS ARE NOT USED TO GUIDE EXECUTION.** Every team maintains separate task lists that are not part of an integrated plan. Project plans are used for budgeting or to track the status of work rather than guide the actual execution.

THE VICIOUS CYCLE

Review the vicious cycle with your team to ensure alignment on the core challenge. Team members have many tasks to perform and the flexibility to select which task to work on (1). Since team members should prioritize their many tasks, they will likely perform tasks in a sequence that will make their work more efficient. Local considerations will play a major role in task prioritization (2). These local considerations are often not aligned with the sequence team members should follow to ensure the timely completion of projects (3). Team members will be under the impression that they are making progress on the project, but eventually, their task selection will cause delays and rework at later stages of the project, typically when work streams are integrated (4). Realizing that projects are delayed, team members will now be under pressure to get started as early as possible to regain productivity (5). This pressure increases the volume of tasks and places even more emphasis on local efficiency considerations (2). The delays and considerable wait times at integration points will incentivize project managers to expedite their tasks by any means possible. They urge the various resource managers to give higher priority to their tasks or work stream (6). For example, they will modify their project plans, so their tasks need to be performed earlier than actually needed. They add duration to their tasks (so it starts earlier), or they create an artificial sequence of activities in their projects so that work is scheduled earlier, gaining priority over other work. This behavior by project managers extends the project lead times and increases the open work in the system. Team members will lose confidence in the project plans and will give more consideration to their own local priorities (2). Team members will start to maintain local task lists and priorities separate from the integrated plan. These local task lists, driven by local metrics, become the primary source of managing execution priorities and schedules. Priorities are no longer aligned with each other or with the global priorities, thereby causing increasing delays. So, the vicious cycle becomes the norm that defines the project's reality.

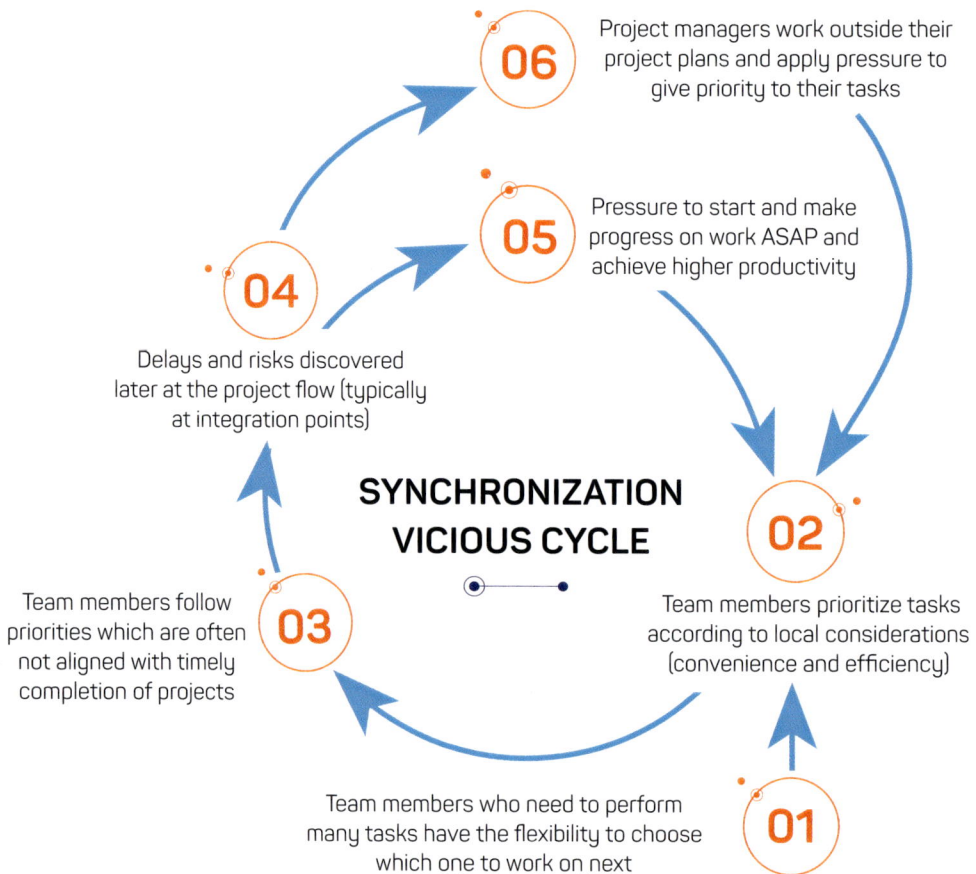

06 Project managers work outside their project plans and apply pressure to give priority to their tasks

05 Pressure to start and make progress on work ASAP and achieve higher productivity

04 Delays and risks discovered later at the project flow (typically at integration points)

SYNCHRONIZATION VICIOUS CYCLE

03 Team members follow priorities which are often not aligned with timely completion of projects

02 Team members prioritize tasks according to local considerations (convenience and efficiency)

01 Team members who need to perform many tasks have the flexibility to choose which one to work on next

THE SOLUTION

To break the vicious cycle and achieve synchronization, we need a mechanism to translate global priorities into aligned local priorities. In a project environment, speed and reliability are of the essence. For example, in a new product development project, speed translates into market share, while reliability allows the business to plan the launch of the product. In a maintenance project, speed translates into asset availability, while reliability allows the usage of the asset to be planned in advance. For a construction project, speed increases the return on the investment, and reliability allows the use of the constructed structure to be planned. The global priorities of a project environment are determined by the aforesaid need for speed and reliability. Local priorities should, therefore, guide team members in selecting the tasks that will support this objective.

What triggers the vicious cycle is that different teams in these environments have many tasks to choose from and the flexibility to make a choice according to their local consideration. A drum is a mechanism for synchronizing priorities throughout the organization by reducing the degrees of freedom (available choices) of the teams that carry out tasks of the project. More specifically, the drum has two functions: (1) it restricts the open WIP of tasks in the system, and (2) it establishes the drumbeat in the organization, the sequence in which the work is performed.

The implementation process of the drum mechanism consists of the following steps:

1 | IDENTIFY A DRUM MECHANISM. Determine the key factor that should dictate the pace and sequence at which work will progress in the system. The mechanism should restrict the amount of WIP and establish a sequence that is aligned with global priorities.

2 | CREATE THE PLAN OF WORK USING A DRUM MECHANISM. The plan should include: A project plan that limits the active WIP of tasks in each project and sequences them in accordance with global priorities.

A pipeline plan reflecting the sequence in which projects would be activated in accordance with the drum mechanism.

3 | ESTABLISH A SINGLE PRIORITY SYSTEM DESIGNED TO IMPROVE FLOW. During the execution phase, local task priorities need to be continually updated based on changes and their impact on project due dates.

Let us elaborate on the above steps.

STEP 1 | IDENTIFY A DRUM MECHANISM
DRUM MECHANISM IN A MULTI-PROJECT ENVIRONMENT

First, consider a multi-project environment where shared resources are working on many active projects.

● In some cases, the mechanism for limiting work in the system, the drum, can be a scarce resource. There are several advantages to setting a scarce resource as the drum. First, since its capacity is less than other resources' capacity, limiting the work in the system so that this scarce resource is not overloaded ensures that all other resources have sufficient capacity. In addition, the resource scarcity ensures that people agree that the system cannot absorb more work and work should be limited. As we limit the work in the system, we should sequence the projects. The factors determining the sequence should be the business priorities and their timelines. For example, in an organization that makes custom automation equipment for customers, the scarce resource is often the experts who have to scope and full-kit the project. These experts are hard to find, and so they naturally limit the WIP in the system. Due-date commitments to customers are the natural prioritization elements. Scarce resources and due dates constitute the drum mechanism. The volume of projects will be limited to the capacity of these experts, and the sequence of projects will be based on the due dates committed to customers.

● In some other cases, it is unclear which resource limits the number of active projects. In this case, it is recommended to set the WIP limit as follows:

● Prioritize the projects in execution.

● Assign resources (e.g., project resources, management resources, experts, etc.) in priority order to ensure that these projects can be completed without any resource shortage. Once resources are insufficient to fully staff a project, it sets the WIP limit.

● This WIP limit can then be adjusted over time based on experience.
The WIP limit of the system, along with the business priorities of the projects, will constitute the drum of the system.

● Sometimes, a phase of a project requires a particular limited capacity or some capital-intensive investment that is not easy to make. In this case, the drum mechanism is the WIP limit of projects in this particular phase, along with the business priorities that will sequence the projects. Take, for example, an assembly bay with all the associated tooling and equipment needed for assembling and testing large complex equipment. In this case, the space limitation of the assembly bay is a natural way to limit the active WIP of projects. The priorities are driven by the due dates of projects. Taken together, the assembly and test phases and the due-date priorities constitute the drum mechanism for projects.

DRUM MECHANISM IN A MULTI-PROJECT ENVIRONMENT

- Release work based on capacity of a scarce resource.
- Sequence work based on business priorities and their timelines.

- Release work based on a full complement of resources to projects.
- Sequence work based on business priorities and their timelines.

- Release work based on limited capacity in a certain project phase.
- Sequence work based on business priorities and their timelines.

DRUM MECHANISM IN A SINGLE-PROJECT ENVIRONMENT

In a single-project environment, there are frequently clear technical dependencies that dictate the sequence of activities in the project. In such cases, the project plan naturally creates the right sequencing of the work and therefore acts as the drum. However, there are cases where the activities sequence is flexible with few technical dependencies. In such cases, there is a need to set a different drum to sequence the activities in the project plan. This can be done as follows:

● In certain projects, such as complex engineering, R&D, or software development, an important mechanism of prioritization and sequencing work is "risk-mitigation". In this context, risk in a project means there is uncertainty about the scope of work to be performed. Often, workers prefer to work first on low-risk activities in order to make progress. They postpone high-risk work, although it has potential to have a big impact on the project. This behavioral pattern leads, in most cases, to significant delays, desynchronization, and costly iterations during the latter phases of the project. Setting risk-mitigation as the prioritization mechanism (the drum) by first doing the high-risk work and later doing lower-risk work is critical to meeting the project's due date and quality commitments. While risk-mitigation sets the sequence of doing the work, we need to augment it with a mechanism to restrict the level of WIP. As in the multi-project case, this can be based on a scarce set of resources, problem-solving capacity, or management bandwidth. In this case, the WIP will be limited to working only on a certain scope of the project. For example, in engineering complex systems such as aircraft and ships, we can limit the WIP by working only on the detailed design of certain segments of the ship at a time or the selected aircraft sections at a time. Such limits, along with sequencing the work based on risk-mitigation can be a powerful drum mechanism to synchronizing priorities.

● In other projects, the major difficulty is the coordination and completion of interdependent work. In this case, the project can be speeded up by restricting the WIP and forcing all functions to coordinate and complete work before proceeding with further work. For example, take a multi-storied building construction project. In such a project, limiting the number of floors on which the different trades (e.g., electrical, plumbing, controls, finishing, painting, etc.) can work forces tight coordination across the trades. This also makes it easier to full-kit, supervise, and synchronize the overall work. The sequence of floors to be worked on is determined by logistical constraints, such as the availability of cranes or elevators.

DRUM MECHANISM IN A SINGLE PROJECT ENVIRONMENT

When activity dependency is fixed:
- Restrict and sequence work based on activities timeline in the project plan.

When activity dependency is flexible & risk is high:
- Restrict work based on scarce capacity.
- Sequence work based on risk-mitigation.

When activity dependency is flexible & coordination of multiple resources is required:
- Define sub-projects and limit the number of active sub-projects.
- Sequence sub-projects based on logical dependencies between them.

Note that to set a drum in a single project, we should define a unit of work - a sub-project (e.g., a floor, a segment of ship/airplane, a cluster of features in software development, etc.). These sub-projects allow us to set WIP limits and sequence the work appropriately in the project plan. We should determine how many sub-projects can be done concurrently and sequence them based on certain criteria. Identifying these sub-projects is critical to set a drum properly in a single project.

STEP 2 | CREATE A PLAN OF WORK USING THE DRUM MECHANISM

Since the sequencing of work in project environments impacts many stakeholders, it is important to develop the project and pipeline plans in a group setting. This is critical to ensure stakeholders buy-in of the drum mechanism (priorities and WIP limits) and its implications for the plan.

PROJECT PLANNING. The drum setting should be at the heart of our project planning, whether it is based on technical dependencies, resource availability or global considerations such as risk-mitigation. The activity network represented in the project plan should reflect the drum. When creating the project plan, it is helpful to keep the following guidelines in mind:

● **START WITH THE PROJECT'S GOAL IN MIND.** What is the project's goal in terms of desired outcome? When defining the goal, ensure it is measurable. This will help clarify the goal. Starting with the goal ensures that every part of the project plan is directly aligned with achieving it. By looking at the goal first, it is easier to identify the specific steps required to achieve it. This method allows project managers to work backwards from the goal, determining what needs to be accomplished just before reaching the goal, and then what needs to happen before that, and so on. This sequence can reveal critical dependencies and prerequisites that might not be apparent when planning starts from the beginning.

● **BREAK THE PROJECT INTO KEY PHASES.** Defining phases in the project plan will help define the key milestones, which can be associated with important decision gates in the project. For example, many projects have a discovery phase at the start of the project. At this stage, one tries to uncover as many unknowns as possible. Once the discovery milestone is completed, important project decisions can be made. Breaking the project into such phases helps define the activities that need to be accomplished to achieve each milestone.

● **WORK BACKWARDS FROM EACH MILESTONE.** Detail the important tasks that need to be achieved for each milestone. A task is a block of work that can be full-kitted and can be executed continually without breaks from start to finish. In general, one should work from a given successor task and build its predecessor's tasks by asking the question: what do we need to achieve in order to start the successor task with all the required inputs? Working backwards in this way helps ensure that the technical dependencies are identified correctly. You may need to break a task into smaller tasks to reflect the right dependencies in the plan.

● **DO NOT OVER DETAIL THE PROJECT PLAN WITH TOO MANY TASKS!** A project plan has multiple purposes. An important one is to act as the project's drum, to determine the sequence of work tasks, and to limit the WIP. Other roles are to define the scope of work, associate the work to the budget, and monitor the progress of work. To act as a drum, the project plan should not be overly detailed. Typically, 100–300 tasks in a project plan are sufficient to sequence the work as a drum. More tasks will hamper synchronization by affording workers the freedom to start earlier tasks that should be deferred until later in the project. When breaking tasks into smaller ones, there may be flexibility to perform each of the small tasks too early, which leads to desynchronization. Naturally, limiting the project plan to fewer tasks does not mean we should not capture important details. Those details can be captured in checklists, sub-projects, job cards, and so on. Another advantage of having a simpler plan is that it is much easier to keep it updated as reality unfolds so that the impact of any change on the project due dates is clearly understood. When the plan is overly detailed, it is difficult to keep all the changes up to date. The plan stops being relevant, and workers ignore it as an execution guide.

● **ADD DURATIONS AND ASSIGN RESPONSIBILITIES.** Once the tasks are defined, assign the worker (or workers) that will be responsible for performing every task and determine each task's duration. When determining such durations, assume that all needed resources are assigned and available and that the execution would proceed smoothly, without disruptions. This will allow you to capture all execution assumptions that should be realized for smooth execution. Estimating the duration of each task this way means that each duration estimate is without a buffer. The buffers will be added to the project plan later on in a consolidated form (see Chapter 9).

● **PICK THE RIGHT WIP LIMIT AND SEQUENCE THE TASKS WITH DEPENDENCIES BASED ON GLOBAL PRIORITIES.** Sometimes, when assigning resources at this stage, we uncover a scarce resource and, therefore, should sequence the work based on this resource's capacity. In other cases, we may need to identify sub-projects and set a WIP limit to restrict the work that can be performed concurrently. As mentioned earlier, this WIP limit is typically set based on a set of scarce resources, problem-solving capacity, or management bandwidth. In sequencing the sub-projects, we need to consider global priorities, such as risk-mitigation, and coordination and integration of multiple workstreams.

● **IDENTIFY THE CRITICAL CHAIN.** Identify the critical chain – the longest chain of dependent activities considering resource dependencies. Managers often have the intuition to identify the critical chain. We should use this intuition to verify that the critical chain coming out of the plan matches their experience. Knowing the critical chain focuses the decision-making in the project. If the critical chain does not meet the desired due date of the project, the team can explore options to increase resources, remove dependencies, or challenge task durations or project scope in order to meet the project goal. This constraint-based planning enables effective decision making since relatively few tasks are on the critical chain.

● **BUFFER THE PLAN.** Add consolidated buffers to protect the critical chain (see Chapter 9).

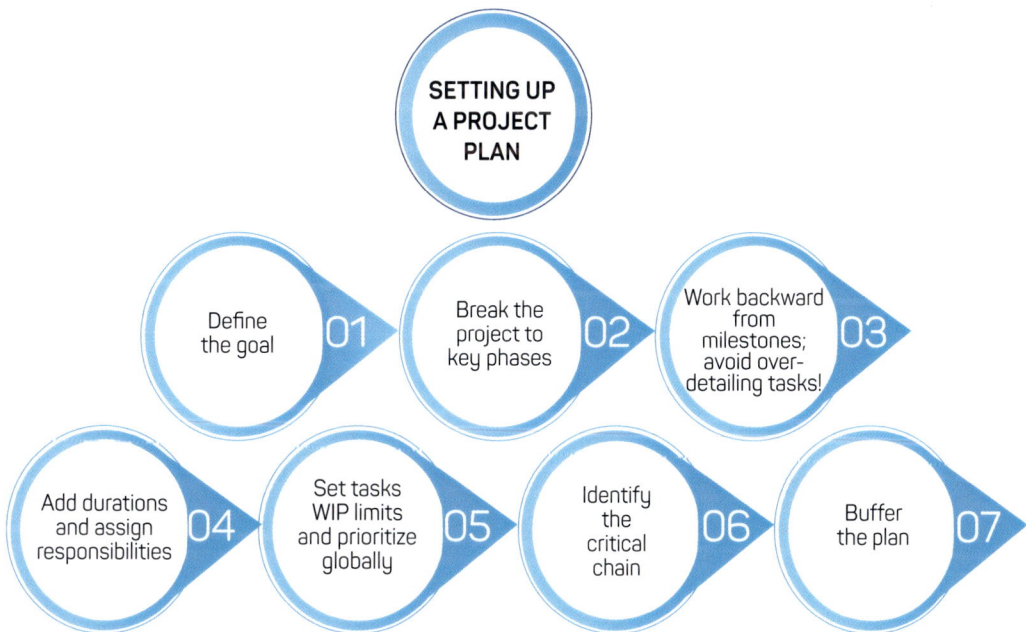

SETTING UP A PROJECT PLAN

01 Define the goal

02 Break the project to key phases

03 Work backward from milestones; avoid over-detailing tasks!

04 Add durations and assign responsibilities

05 Set tasks WIP limits and prioritize globally

06 Identify the critical chain

07 Buffer the plan

PIPELINE PLANNING. In a multi-project environment, the simplest drum mechanism is to set a limit for the number of active projects and determine their sequence based on some prioritization criteria. When building a project pipeline plan, we start with the list of projects and estimates of their durations. We then design a pipeline that has slots corresponding to the WIP limit. The pipeline plan is constructed by slotting these projects into the WIP slots. Once slotted, projects can be systematically introduced into the workflow, allowing us to set realistic deadlines as per the drum schedule. Consider the example of assembling complex equipment. We establish a WIP limit that corresponds to the assembly bay's capacity, which can accommodate four projects simultaneously. We start by prioritizing our current project list to decide which four projects to launch first. As each project has a predefined duration, this helps us schedule the start of subsequent projects, such as the fifth one, and so on. The availability of a slot in the assembly bay's schedule determines the project's start time. Having a properly buffered project plan allows us to reliably set projects' due dates.

WIP LIMIT = 4

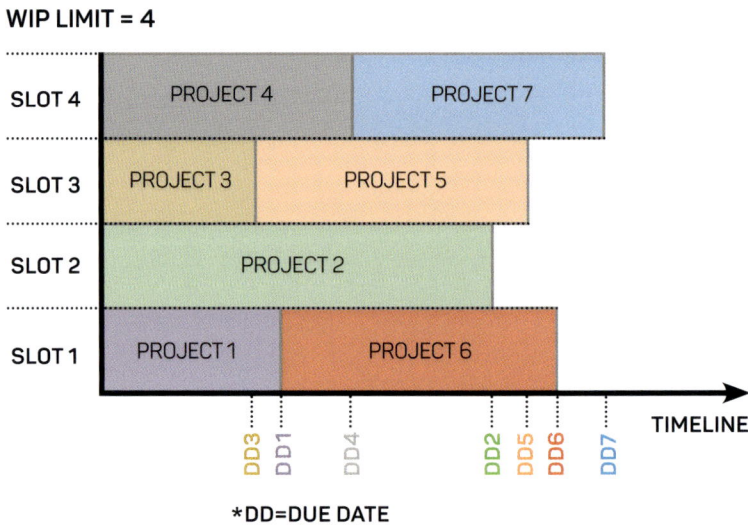

*DD=DUE DATE

This methodology enables us to create a single priority system based on due dates. Projects are scheduled in available WIP slots based on their importance, and their due dates are set according to the drum's schedule and project's duration. From this point onwards, the project's related task priorities will only be determined based on their impact on completing the projects by their due dates.

STEP 3 | **ESTABLISH A SINGLE PRIORITY SYSTEM**

Regardless of how good the plan is, changes in projects are a reality. The project plan must be continually updated to reflect changes in scope, resource availability, timelines, etc. It is critical to keep the plan up to date so that it reflects reality; otherwise, workers will ignore it. As mentioned earlier, this is another reason to keep the plan simple (100–300 activity blocks). The plan must be used to assess the impact of the changes on the project's timeline, and to reach agreements on required mitigation actions.

In execution, the local priorities are determined with a mindset of speeding up project workflows. Tasks will receive higher priority based on the impact of their completion on the project's due date. There are simple ways to calculate this impact and generate a priority list based on the risk of project delays by tasks with tardy completion dates. Tasks on the longest chain of dependencies have a higher priority, and those with more slack have a lower priority. This mechanism is revisited in greater detail in Chapter 9. The buffer becomes the mechanism for managing changes and priorities during project execution.

HOW TO CAUSE THE CHANGE

Several obstacles may block our ability to effectively apply the synchronization solution:

● **LOCAL EFFICIENCY METRICS.** Often in project environments, teams are measured on local task commitments, such as the need to accomplish a volume of work in a certain time, or task-level due dates. All such metrics have to be abolished to enable synchronization. People should be held accountable for executing the tasks in such a way that there is minimal buffer wastage, and not held accountable to meeting local tasks commitments.

● **BUY-IN ON PLANS.** Network building for a project is critical in overcoming this obstacle. Building a project plan with all stakeholders is critical to achieving their buy-in of the plan and its underlying assumptions. In a similar vein, reaching agreement on the drum mechanism in a multi-project environment is critical.

● **INERTIA.** Workers are worried about losing their freedom to make decisions. In reality, working with buffers, they are capable of making better decisions to solve problems seeing the impact on global performance. Understanding this connection with clarity greatly empowers workers.

GUIDING QUESTIONS FOR GROUP DISCUSSION & IMPLEMENTATION

Follow these guiding questions to facilitate a discussion with your team on getting synchronization right in your project flow:

NEED FOR BETTER SYNCHRONIZATION

1 Are there significant waiting times and rework at integration points in projects?

2 How relevant are the list of indicators and the vicious cycle?

SETTING UP A DRUM TO SYNCHRONIZE RESOURCES ACROSS MULTIPLE PROJECTS

3 Are there scarce resources that will dictate the number of projects in WIP? What should be the WIP limit?

4 Starting with the highest priority projects, once we assign the needed resources, how many projects can be in WIP?

5 Is there a phase in the projects that should dictate the number of projects running concurrently? What should be the limit?

6 What global considerations should determine the sequence of projects released to WIP?

SETTING UP A DRUM TO SYNCHRONIZE RESOURCES IN A SINGLE PROJECT

7 Are there many tasks in the project plan that aren't sequenced by technical dependencies?

8 What are the right sub-projects that will determine the WIP work limit?

9 Will there likely be late discovery of risk in the project? If so, should we sequence tasks based on risk mitigation?

10 How should we sequence the sub-projects to minimize the duration of the project? For example, should we start with big sub-projects first and then do the small ones? Should we consider the availability of certain critical resources?

ALIGNING PROJECTS AND PIPELINE PLANS

11 Are the project plans constructed with a clear task sequence that supports the timely completion of projects?

12 Is the buffer aggregated to protect the project's flow (see Chapter 9)?

13 Does the project pipeline plan include clear restrictions on WIP and criteria for sequencing project releases into WIP based on business priorities?

AGGREGATE & MANAGE
TIME BUFFERS

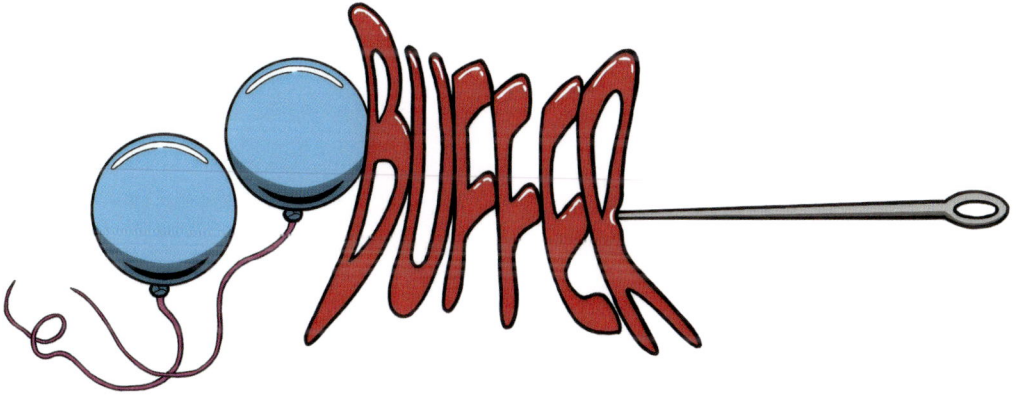

While addressing the obstacles to flow increases productivity and reduces variability, uncertainty still remains a significant factor in project work. Rather than trying to eliminate variability completely, we should strive to construct a system to achieve our objectives in the face of variability. Incorporating time buffers in our processes is essential for managing workflow and ensuring reliable performance. These buffers play a pivotal role in mitigating the impact of disruptions and upholding commitments. Time buffers absorb potential delays to prevent missed deadlines. Without these buffers, tasks often become urgent, disrupting flow.

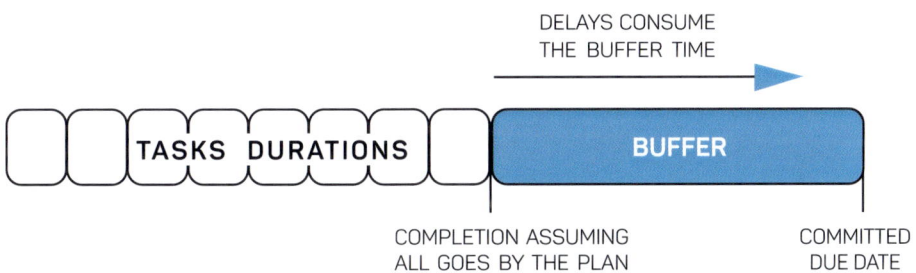

DELAYS CONSUME
THE BUFFER TIME

TASKS DURATIONS   BUFFER

COMPLETION ASSUMING
ALL GOES BY THE PLAN

COMMITTED
DUE DATE

The main challenge Is in the sizing of the buffers. Excessively large buffers lead to extended lead times and increased budgets, whereas buffers that are too small fail to provide sufficient due-date protection.

In most project environments, team members believe that buffer time is insufficient. If it weren't for time pressures, they would add safety margins of time to meet their deadlines, especially in the face of high levels of uncertainty. This belief engenders a vicious cycle. Since team members think there isn't enough buffer (3), they aim to start and hand off tasks as quickly as possible, operating under the assumption that starting early means finishing early (4). This rush to begin and hand off work as soon as possible leads to an overwhelming number of tasks and hectic, bad multitasking (5). Additionally, much of the work progresses without being fully kitted, causing frequent issues (6). Consequently, delays and rework become the norm (7). Understandably, this reinforces the impression that there is not enough buffer, perpetuating the cycle.

This perception not only engenders a vicious cycle but also leads us to believe that the only solution is to add more buffers. Since this is infeasible due to time pressures, as

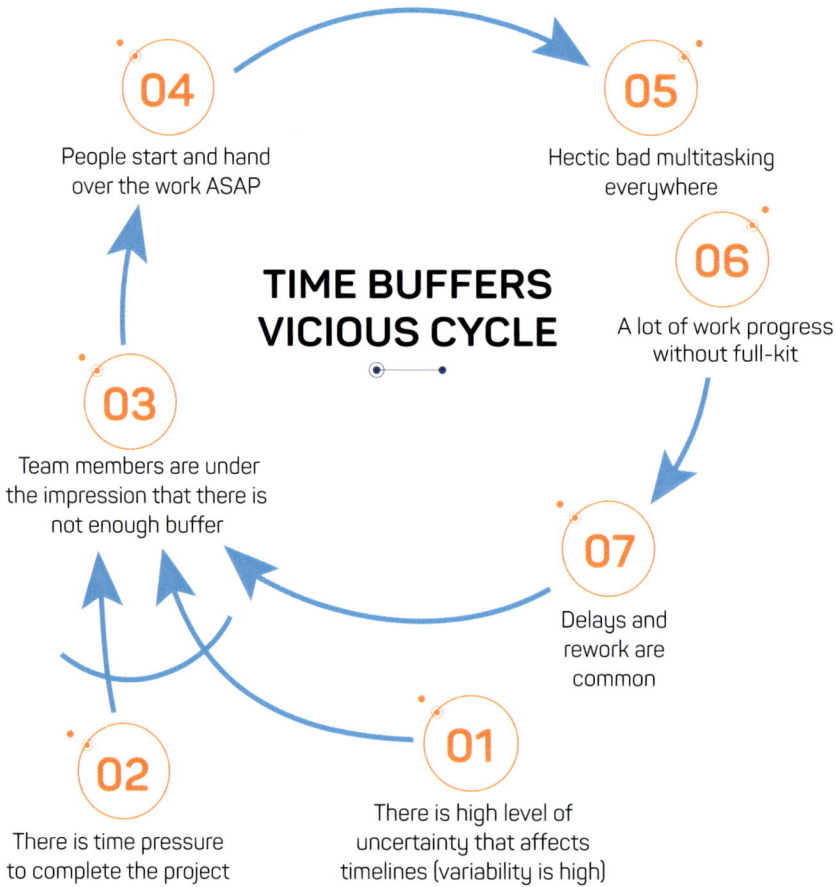

TIME BUFFERS VICIOUS CYCLE

04 — People start and hand over the work ASAP

05 — Hectic bad multitasking everywhere

06 — A lot of work progress without full-kit

03 — Team members are under the impression that there is not enough buffer

07 — Delays and rework are common

02 — There is time pressure to complete the project

01 — There is high level of uncertainty that affects timelines (variability is high)

long as we continue to think that way, we are trapped in a vicious cycle. To break it, we need to challenge the belief that the existing buffers are insufficient despite experience suggesting otherwise. The solution does not lie in hoping to get more buffers but rather in using the existing ones more efficiently.

AGGREGATING BUFFERS

Typically, we incorporate buffers into the plan by adding a "safety time" to each estimated task duration. For example, say we plan 4 tasks, and each one, under normal circumstances, should take ten days to complete. Since many things can go off plan, we add a buffer to each task estimation (e.g., in this case, each task will be planned to take 15–20 days). For the reasons explained below, a much better option is not to allocate such "safety time" to each task but to use a consolidated unallocated buffer for use by all tasks. In our example, we will plan each task to take ten days and have a consolidated unallocated buffer of just

20 days. Team members should strive to complete tasks within planned timelines that do not include a buffer. When disruptions increase tasks durations beyond their planned values, the consolidated buffer is utilized.

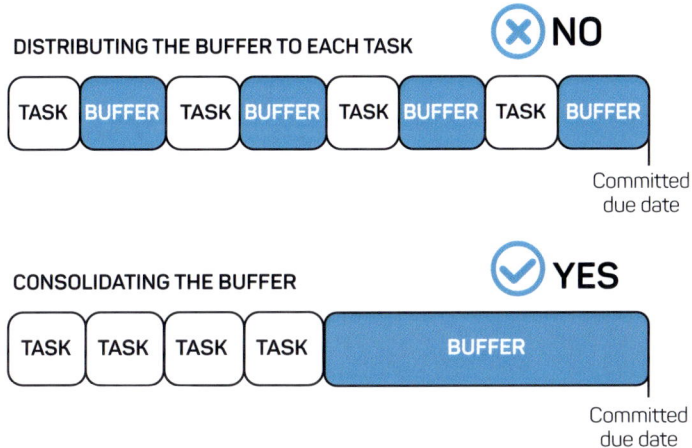

DISTRIBUTING THE BUFFER TO EACH TASK ⊗ **NO**

| TASK | BUFFER | TASK | BUFFER | TASK | BUFFER | TASK | BUFFER |

Committed
due date

CONSOLIDATING THE BUFFER ✓ **YES**

| TASK | TASK | TASK | TASK | BUFFER |

Committed
due date

There are several reasons why we should use consolidated buffers when creating the project plan rather than allocating separate buffers for each individual task:

1 | A high level of uncertainty implies that we cannot predict when and where delays will occur. If we decide to allocate the buffers upfront to protect each task separately, we will need a bigger buffer to provide protection to all of them. Having a consolidated general buffer and using it only when and where needed will enable us to provide the same level of protection with a considerably smaller buffer.

2 | A high level of uncertainty can occasionally result in big disruptions causing significant delays. When allocating buffers to protect each task, there will be insufficient buffer to protect against such delays. A consolidated buffer creates a much bigger pool of protection than any individual task buffer.

3 | One main benefit of using a consolidated buffer is that it helps prevent wasting our valuable buffers. Adding buffers to each task's timeline can lead to exhausting them too soon, often before they are actually needed. This unnecessary use of buffers is typically driven by common behavioral patterns:

● **Parkinson's Law** posits that "work expands to occupy the time allotted for its completion." This principle suggests that people regulate their pace of work to meet the deadlines set.

If workers are consistently busy, yet under crisis situations, they can complete the job much faster, it indicates the presence of Parkinson's Law.

● **Student Syndrome** describes a procrastination pattern, where people delay starting their work, leading to a "hockey stick" pattern of workload distribution. Initially, there is minimal activity, but as the deadline draws near, work effort sharply increases, and one then observes a burst of intense work just before the deadline. Such behavior often leads to wasting buffer time early on, which will be sorely needed during the last-minute rush to complete the task.

● **Delayed reporting.** In some cases, task managers delay reporting early completion because they worry that it might backfire and set a precedent. They worry that setting expectations for quicker task completion would now make it difficult to add extra time in future estimates.

● **Fixed schedules.** When various resources are assigned to consecutive tasks in a project plan, this can result in inefficient use of buffers. Adding a buffer to the time estimate for the initial task delays the start of the next task. If the initial task is completed early, the resources for the next task may not be ready to begin earlier. Consequently, the team that completed the first task might see no benefit in speeding up the work handoff. Thus, the buffer time is used up whether or not it is needed.

● **Tasks integration.** A similar phenomenon often occurs when multiple concurrent tasks need to be completed before the next task can start. That is, at such integration points in the project flow, if one of the predecessor tasks is completed early, the successor task cannot start till all other predecessor tasks are completed. In such a scenario, the resources performing the predecessor tasks realize that being early will not make a difference. They also know that the likelihood of all predecessor tasks finishing early is probably nil, and therefore, they work to finish at the planned due date (which includes a buffer). Again, the buffers are wasted because they are used even when not needed.

The reasons above explain why aggregating the "safety time" allocated to each task into a general consolidated buffer will ensure that we have sufficient buffer time to mitigate most disruptions. The consolidated buffer should be positioned at the end of the critical chain - the longest chain of dependent tasks when considering resource contingencies.

HOW DO YOU CREATE AN EFFECTIVE CONSOLIDATED BUFFER?

The Theory of Constraints does not support overly precise long-term projections, particularly in environments characterized by high levels of uncertainty. Attempting to impose certainty on uncertain situations may well give rise to a false sense of security. Instead of trying to precisely estimate buffer sizes, it is better to make a reasonable estimate that covers common disruptions and set up mechanisms for their quick detection and recovery. What is considered a reasonable buffer size? As a rule of thumb, having a consolidated buffer equal to one-third of the planned project duration should be more than sufficient.

The consolidated buffer should be created by excluding the "safety times" currently incorporated into estimated task durations. People generally want to honor their commitments and avoid missing deadlines. Therefore, given the high uncertainty and frequent challenges in workflows, experienced workers will make an estimate with a 50% buffer to ensure they can deliver on time. Does this appear excessive? To answer this question, a quick thought exercise is in order. To this end, assume a perfect world with no disruptions or variability where a certain task takes two weeks to complete. Now, back to the real world, where there is much variability, many things can go wrong, priorities are constantly shifting, and necessary inputs are often missing; how long do you estimate the task will take? Keeping in mind that your estimation will turn into a commitment, would you commit to two weeks? Two weeks plus one day? Two weeks plus two days? Would it perhaps be three weeks? Most likely, for your estimate to be reliable, your gut feeling, backed up by painfully earned experience, tells you that you had better commit to close to four weeks, two of which are a buffer.

It is recommended to plan tasks at half their current estimated durations and move the saved time into a consolidated buffer. As previously explained, allocating buffers to each individual task requires more total "safety times" than using a consolidated buffer. Note that the consolidated buffer does not actually need all the "safety times" extracted from each task's duration estimate. In fact, it is common to use only half of the extracted total time. The project is planned with each task duration equal to only 50% of initial estimation, and 50% of the total extracted "safety times" is allocated to the consolidated buffer for protecting the entire critical chain. Effectively, the consolidated buffer will then equal one-third of the new, much shorter project lead time.

For example, consider a project with four tasks, where under the usual planning method, each task is estimated to take 12 days. Remember that each of these task estimations includes a six-day buffer. The total project duration is 48 days. Using the recommended consolidated buffer approach, each task should be planned for six days. The "safety time" extracted totals 24 days (4 tasks x 6 days). However, we don't need all 24 days for the consolidated buffer; 12 days (50% of the extracted time) would suffice. This new approach reduces the total project duration from 48 days to 36 days, with 12 days (1/3 of the total) serving as the consolidated buffer.

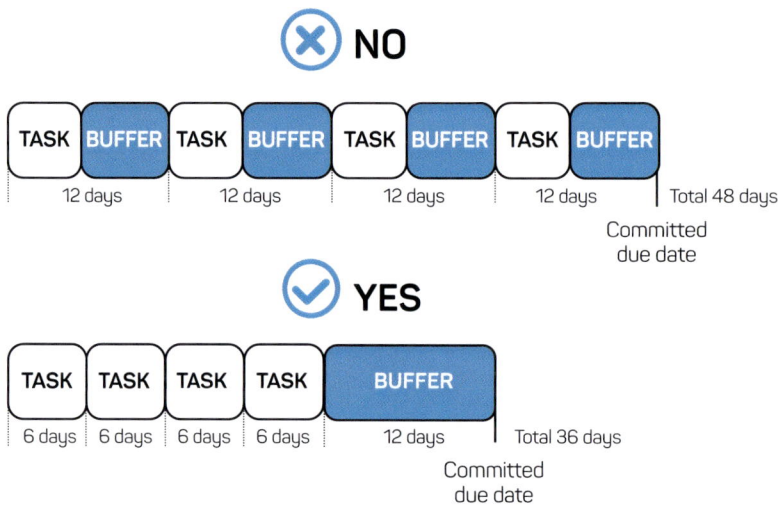

Extracting buffer time from each task's estimated duration would naturally raise concerns among those accountable for performing the tasks. Holding them accountable to complete tasks in half the time of their original buffered estimates may seem extremely risky. Some may even insist that there is no "safety time" whatsoever in the plan. There are several tactics that can be used to address such concerns and gain genuine collaboration:

1 | Be very explicit that there is a buffer when needed. Build the confidence that although workers should strive to complete their tasks on time, when delays occur, there will be a buffer to draw on. In fact, it is expected that the buffer will be consumed by various disruptions throughout the lifetime of the project.

2 | Gain credibility by demonstrating that it is possible to complete tasks much faster. First remove the dominant obstacles to flow to demonstrate that tasks can be completed much faster without the need for 50% buffer time.

3 | Perform a POC to demonstrate the new approach. If possible, select a representative project or a project phase, and demonstrate that when the obstacles to flow are addressed, it is possible to complete the project on plan (or even earlier) by instituting a consolidated buffer without "safety time" embedded in planned durations of the tasks.

4 | Start with a bigger consolidated buffer as extra protection. Should team members have concerns about the shift in buffer allocation, you can opt to start the project with a bigger consolidated buffer. Keep in mind, that the key change is to strip individual tasks of their "safety time" margins, but providing an ample consolidated buffer, still without prolonging the overall project duration. As the team observes projects being completed ahead of schedule, they will gain the confidence needed to decrease the consolidated buffer.

5 | Utilize simulations and exercises. Having workers experience the impact of new methodologies through simulations and group exercises is very powerful. Use an exercise to demonstrate the power of removing obstacles to flow. See *Goldratt's Rules of Flow* for an example of such a game.

You can use the following technique to extract the buffers from the task estimations and create a consolidated buffer:

● Establish a baseline performance that corresponds to the current situation with the prevailing obstacles to flow, where workers experience many disruptions (e.g., six months).

● Agree with the team that removing the dominant obstacles to flow in their environment can enable faster work completion, say 25% improvement (i.e., 4.5 months). Note that you may need to do a POC or run some exercises for the team to accept this logic. For example, you can simulate how fast the team can complete the job if everything is ready and priorities are kept unchanged, etc.

● Ask task managers for their estimates of improved project duration under the assumption that improvement is possible, and the project can be completed within 75% of the lead time (e.g., they will fit it into 4.5 months).

● To better manage the buffer, remove one-third of each task duration estimate and aggregate the removed times to form the consolidated buffer. Note, since the task estimate is subject to the assumption that the task duration variability has already been reduced, we don't need to extract half of the estimated time and then cut the total extracted time by half. Rather, we agree to extract one-third of each task duration estimate and aggregate all extracted times into a consolidated buffer that will be available when needed.

It would be easier for task managers to accept such a change as a gradual process rather than to be asked to extract 50% of their task duration estimates and then take only 50% of the extracted time as a buffer.

Important note: once the obstacles to flow are addressed, we achieve much better performance, and delays are less common. Eventually team members will include shorter "safety times" in their task duration estimates. At this point, instead of cutting task duration estimates by 50%, when creating the plan, we should reduce them by a smaller margin, or use historical data showing the actual, much shorter completion times for similar tasks. Remember, as a general rule of thumb, the buffer should be equal to one-third of the total project duration.

ESTABLISHING A BUFFER MANAGEMENT MECHANISM FOR FAST RESPONSE

Having a mechanism to quickly identify disruptions that draw upon the buffer is crucial for buffer recovery. Such a mechanism acts as a dashboard, helping management prioritize and speed up projects at risk of missing deadlines while there is still buffer time available to realign the project with its schedule. The buffer management mechanism monitors the progress along the critical chain and compares it to the amount of buffer used thus far. To facilitate this, task managers should frequently update the "remaining durations" of their respective tasks - the estimated times to complete each task.

Should a task's expected completion time exceed its planned duration, the buffer would be reduced by the difference. For example, in the following figure, "Task 1" was originally scheduled to complete in five days. Due to unforeseen delays, the task manager notified that it is now expected to take ten days. Hence, the buffer is effectively reduced (consumed) by five days.

A red flag is raised when the progress on the critical chain is too small relative to the amount of buffer consumed. Focusing on expediting the project can recover lost buffer time. For

PLAN

REALITY

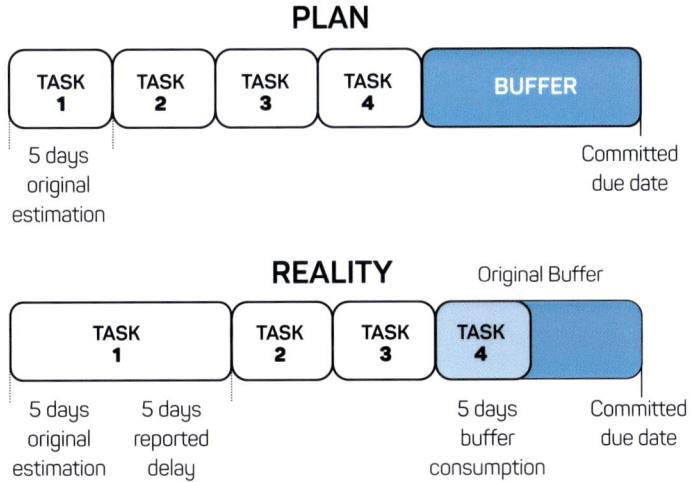

instance, when the manager of Task 1 indicated a delay, revising the task's expected duration from 5 to 10 days, swift measures to counteract this delay can realign the task with its original schedule, thereby recovering the 5 days of buffer that was consumed.

The chart below, commonly known as a *Fever Chart*, depicts the progress on the critical chain of a specific project along the X-axis, against the percentage of buffer consumed, as shown on the Y-axis.

The color zones represent the likelihood of completing the project on time considering

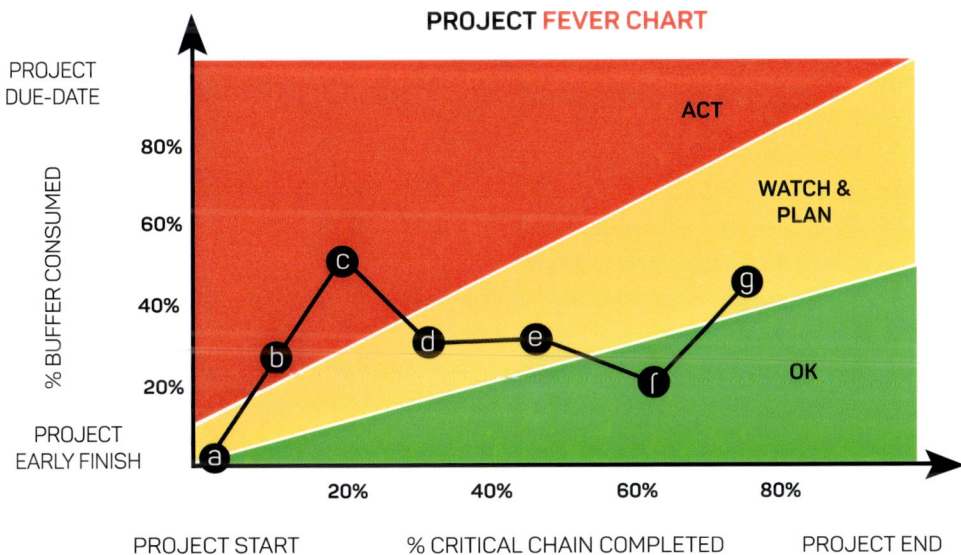

PROJECT FEVER CHART

the progress made on the critical chain relative to the remaining buffer time. Specifically, a green status means that progress is satisfactory, a yellow status means unsatisfactory meriting alert, and a red status means that the project is in a critically poor condition and, absent remedial actions, the project is not likely to be completed on time. We should design the slopes, dividing the color zones to enable early warnings when the rate of buffer consumption is too high relative to the progress made on the critical chain.[4] For example, point **a** on the graph shows about 5% completion of the critical chain and about 1% of the buffer consumed. At this early stage, the project is on track, showcasing a satisfactory balance between progress and buffer consumption, which places it in the green **OK** zone. However, at point **b**, the situation shifts; although only 16% of the critical chain has been completed, the buffer consumption has risen to 24%. This disparity signals a move into the red zone, where the rate of buffer consumption relative to progress is a cause for concern and necessitates immediate remedial action to avoid project delays. As the project progresses to point **c**, the project's scenario deteriorates further, with just 20% of the critical chain completed, whereas nearly half (50%) of the buffer has been consumed, which requires urgent measures to speed up project progress.

The graph then demonstrates a turnaround at point **d**, where, thanks to successful intervention, the project has advanced to 35% completion of the critical chain, with just under 30% of the buffer being consumed. Note that the buffer consumption went from 50% to 30%. This can occur when tasks are completed more quickly than originally estimated, or when we successfully reduced the reported, extended remaining duration estimates. This marks a transition to the yellow phase—a **Watch and Plan** stage, where we still need to be on alert, making sure the project does not deteriorate and fall back into the red.

Note that buffers should be regarded as a highly valuable resource. Even when a project appears to be on track (green status), it is important to ensure that the buffer is not

---

[4] There are different ways to determine the slopes dividing the color zones. The general logic is to turn a project to a red status early enough to provide recovery time. The general rule of thumb is to divide the percent of Buffer Consumed (%BC) by the percent of Critical Chain Completion (%CCC), with the following logic: if %BC/%CCC < 1, then it is green; if %BC/%CCC is approximately 1 then yellow; if %BC/%CCC > 1, then it is red.

being consumed prematurely. As described in this book, team members might engage in multitasking, neglect to fully prepare for tasks, deviate from the plan for localized reasons, provide smaller work dosages to tackle more tasks, etc. It is the responsibility of project managers to oversee task execution and ask tough questions when they notice that the buffer is over-consumed. This should be done even if the project's status is green. Staying vigilant and promoting the correct behaviors and maintaining a disciplined workflow are essential. Managing buffers effectively is a powerful tool for project execution.

MONITORING PROJECT STATUS IN THIS MANNER OFFERS SEVERAL KEY BENEFITS:

● **Early warning for timely recovery.** Early detection of red flags allows for timely intervention. Traditional methods might only signal issues after the buffer is entirely consumed, leaving little room for corrective action. However, by comparing buffer consumption with progress on the critical chain, projects can be flagged as being at risk (red zone) much earlier, even during the initial stages. Such an early warning system enables timely recovery measures to meet original deadlines.

● **Prioritization based on global project health.** This approach allows for the strategic prioritization of tasks across projects. Critical chain tasks within projects that are in the red zone, indicating a high risk of delay, can be given priority over those in projects that are on track (green zone). Setting priorities in this way emphasizes the importance of maintaining project flow and global efficiency over local optimizations.

● **Collaboration on the critical chain mode of planning.** Knowing that there is a support system in place for reporting as well as addressing delays, task managers will be more inclined to plan projects with a consolidated unallocated buffer rather than individual task buffers.

● **Enhanced reliability of what-if scenarios.** Tracking the ratio of buffer consumption to critical chain progress allows management to better predict the outcomes of various decisions. For example, such tracking can help determine whether to reallocate resources to other projects, open new projects as planned, cut scope or tasks, change the sequence of tasks, etc. By analyzing how quickly the buffer is consumed relative to progress on the critical chain across projects, management can make informed decisions about the potential impact of such actions on the completion of the overall project portfolio.

SIMPLIFIED BUFFER MANAGEMENT MECHANISM

In certain cases, we can simplify the buffer management process by not requiring task managers to estimate and report remaining task durations. There are project environments where the variability in the actual time it takes to perform the tasks is not extremely high. The delays and uncertainty in these environments stem more from work settings (e.g., team availability) and competing priorities across projects and less from the actual time it takes to do each task. Since in such environments, the variability of actual task duration is not high; it is often possible to speed up task completions and complete projects on time, even with only one-third of the buffer remaining. Accordingly, we can set the color zones in the fever chart to three equal one-third buffer zones. In that case, we ask task managers to report only when a task is complete without reporting the remaining durations. When delays occur on the critical chain, the delays consume buffer time. The project is considered "green" and on track as long as the buffer consumed is within the first third of the allocated time. It turns Yellow when more than 1/3 of the buffer is consumed. A "red" status is assigned when two-thirds of the buffer time has been consumed, and we have not yet completed the project.

This buffer management mechanism simplifies project monitoring by focusing on actual versus expected progress without requiring task managers to constantly report on remaining durations. Typically, when the variability of actual task duration is not high, we can further simplify the planning process and create project templates with the activity networks, timelines, and buffers.

The following figure depicts three scenarios of a project. The first scenario is the plan. In the second scenario, two tasks got delayed and consumed less than one-third of the buffer - the project is green. In the third scenario, the additional delay caused the consumption of more than one-third but less than two-thirds of the buffer - the project turned yellow. Note that in this simplified version, we only track the buffer consumption according to the actual reports on tasks completion.

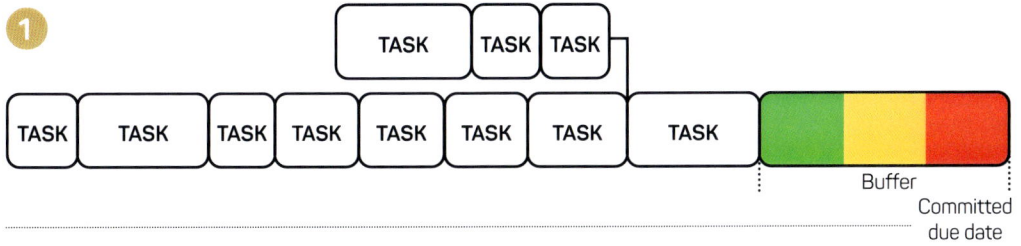

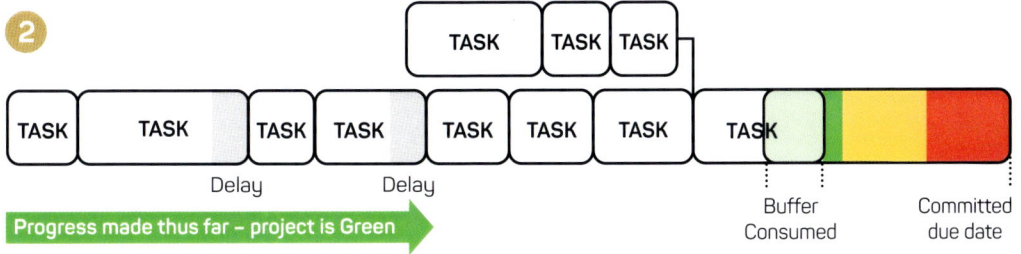

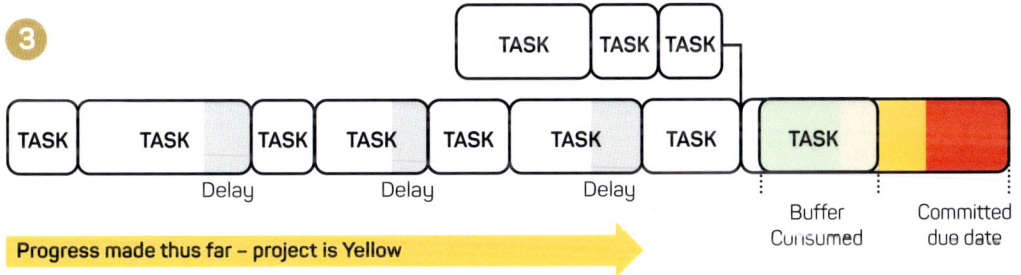

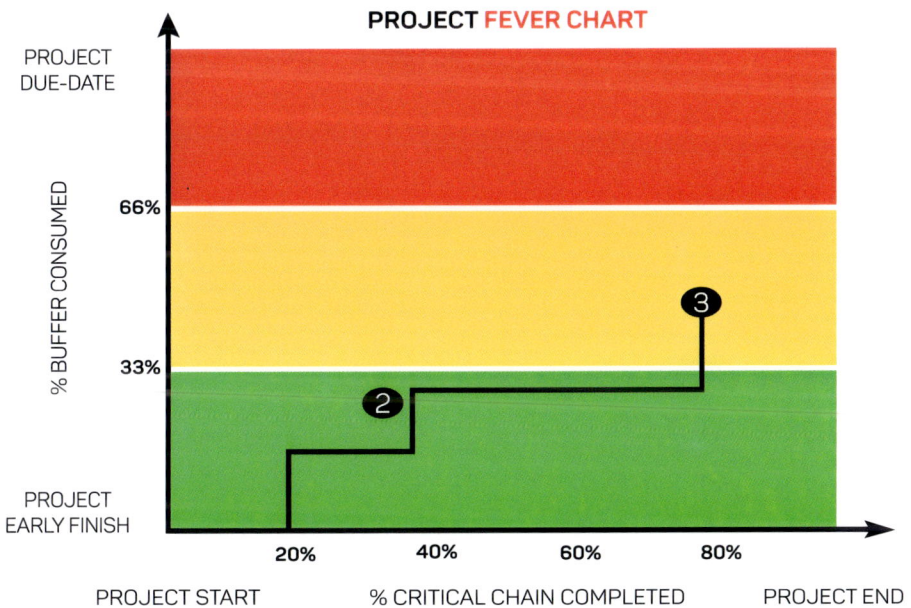

IDENTIFYING CAUSES FOR DELAYS | A PROCESS OF ONGOING IMPROVEMENT

The buffer management mechanism can be used to gather data and focus improvement efforts on the current most common causes of delay. It can be implemented in the following manner:

● Whenever a task manager reports a delay, record the reason for the delay. Ask the question: What is the work waiting for? The answer can be a certain input (e.g., materials, information, or authorization), availability of a certain resource, or incomplete rework. Make sure the answers are recorded in a consistent manner to enable analysis (it is recommended to create simplified drop-down menu options).

● When a project drops into the red zone, gather all the reasons for the delays that brought it to the red zone.

● If the delay persists, repeat recording the reason every set time interval (e.g., a time equal to 10% of the project duration) for as long as the project remains in the red zone.

● When conducting the analysis, identify the most common cause across projects that have reached a red status.

● Focus improvement efforts to resolve that cause in a consistent manner.

● Measure success to ensure that the cause was dealt with properly and is no longer the most common one.

GUIDING QUESTIONS FOR GROUP DISCUSSION & IMPLEMENTATION

Discuss these questions with your team prior to implementing time buffers in your project flow:

1 How much "safety time" do people add to task duration estimates?
Remember:

● The bigger the disruptions, the bigger the "safety time" added.

● If you have already tackled the dominant obstacles to flow and witnessed a significant reduction in task completion times, you can re-estimate the durations under the improved scenario.

● The consolidated buffer should be one-third of the total planned project duration.

● You may need to simplify the plan to embed the aggregated buffer. Don't let the plan go over 300 tasks (see Chapter 8).

2 How to track buffer consumption during project execution?
Remember: If there is high variability in task durations, you should ask for the remaining duration. Otherwise, you can just track actual task completion times.

3 How early do you need a warning to ensure the project completes on time?
Remember: According to your answer, you should determine the ratio of buffer consumption to critical chain completion, which will turn the project's status red.

4 How to ensure that buffer times are not wasted?
Remember: the buffer is a highly valuable asset. Even if the project is green, you should put in place mechanisms to make sure that buffer times are not wasted.

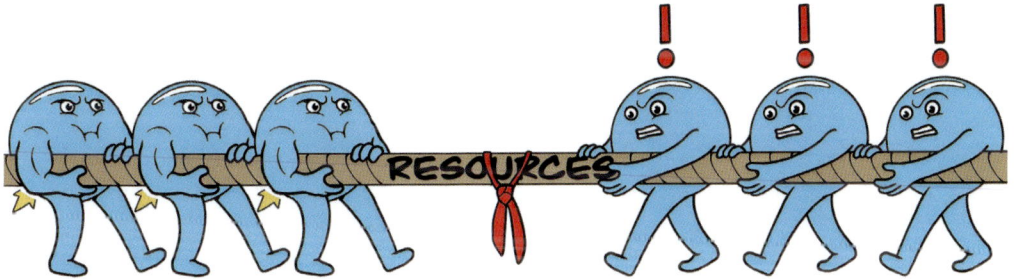

10
CHAPTER

POOL
RESOURCES

OBSTACLES TO FLOW

The demand for certain resources in a project rises and falls.[5] Sometimes, these resources are segmented for specific projects, so they can't be utilized for other projects - even when they have the capacity to do so.

EXAMPLES

Maintenance technicians at an Air Force base hosting multiple squadrons. Often there are multiple squadrons of the same aircraft platform positioned at the same Air Force base. Each squadron is equipped with a full team of maintenance specialists (avionics, airframe, hydraulics, electrical, etc.) to ensure self-sufficiency and readiness for deployment with a full complement of resoruces for forward operations. While serveral squadrons are at the Air Force base, one may need more technician capacity while the other has technicians available. This segmentation creates bottlenecks, leading to delays and lower aircraft availability as aircraft remain grounded waiting for repairs. Reduced aircraft availability impacts the number of training flights pilots can complete, directly affecting mission readiness.

Telecom software company providing billing and customer management software to telecommunication companies. The software company's customers shifted the terms of engagement from time-and-material to fixed-price contracts, meaning the vendor must absorb any extra hours beyond the fixed budget. This puts pressure on margins as the cost risks of doing technology upgrade projects now falls on the software company. To control costs the software company moved towards creating a matrix organization where

---

[5] In this book the term 'resources' refers to all the elements the organization employs in order to achieve its goals. In project environments the most valuable resources are often not the organization's physical resources such as equipment and materials, but rather, the human resources, the organization's experts and technicians. For the sake of simplicity, we also refer to all the professionals involved in the projects as recourses.

resources were shared across projects. This would allow resource utilization to be higher while in theory not harming project delivery. In reality managing the conflict over scarce resources was difficult with project managers complaining about not having the resources to deliver, while resource managers tried to have just the right capacity of resources to support the projects and stay within the budgets. As a result, projects were delayed, budgets were overrun, and the company's reputation for reliable delivery was threatened.

Experts in a startup that is growing fast. A medical device startup transitioning from prototyping to commercialization is developing various product variations to address different disease endpoints. These devices and their manufacturing processes must comply with regulatory requirements in different markets. Expert resources are spread across multiple projects, providing guidance to resolve technical challenges and ensure regulatory compliance. However, when these experts are unavailable, projects slow down due to delays in issue resolution and decision-making.

Engineers in an aerospace OEM. Resources need to be assigned to projects so that they are not on overhead. This reality puts pressure on resources to be assigned to projects at all times. It often means that resources are not fully available where they are needed resulting in projects delays. At the same time, underutilized resources on other projects start work before the design is matured and all assumptions are clarified, leading to rework and iterations.

THE CHALLENGE

In projects the workload on resources is not spread evenly through the life of the project. Sometimes the project has peaks and valleys in the need for resources. For example, in an engineering project the system engineers, system architects, business analysts, experienced experts are needed mainly at the start of the project. In maintenance projects inspectors are needed towards the start and operators towards the end when the systems are brought back online. In construction projects heavy-earth-moving equipment is needed at the start of the project and finishing resources towards the end of the project. The peaks and valleys can also emerge out of the uncertainties in project work. For example, experts may be called upon at any time to fix issues and make critical decisions. Emergent peaks and valleys compound the problem of planning and allocating resources. It is challenging in these environments to staff to the peaks in all projects. As a result, often there are resource shortages where resources are not available as needed. For this reason, project managers, who are accountable for on-time performance often favor having dedicated resources to their projects. Sometimes when the projects are organized into many small portfolios each portfolio manager looks to have dedicated resources. This creates a challenge in resource management. On one hand resources are not available as needed, on the other hand resources can be underutilized. The challenge of organizing resources often leads organizations to oscillate between pooling resources to improve efficiency or isolate them by project to eliminate excuses for delays and increase project managers' accountability.

INDICATORS

How to tell if resources are over segmented in your projects resulting in delays and inefficiencies. Check if the following indicators are common issues faced by the team:

● **RESOURCES ARE NOT AVAILABLE WHEN NEEDED.** Once segmented to projects it is not easy to utilize these resources for other projects that are understaffed.

● **RESOURCES ASSIGNED TO A PROJECT NEED TO BE REASSIGNED TO RECOVER FROM DELAYS IN ANOTHER PROJECT.** When delays occur, companies often need to shift resources between projects to prevent cascading setbacks. However, reassigning resources disrupts the original project's workflow.

● **PROJECTS ARE DELAYED AND PROJECT MANAGERS COMPLAIN ABOUT BEING HELD ACCOUNTABLE TO COMMITMENTS THAT THEY CANNOT CONTROL.** Project managers are expected to meet due-dates, but when key resources are unavailable or constantly reassigned, they struggle to keep commitments. They face pressure to deliver results despite unpredictable setbacks caused by competing demands on shared resources.

● **RESOURCES FACE PEAKS AND VALLEYS. WORK MOVES IN WAVES WITH PERIODS OF LOW PRESSURE FOLLOWED BY LONG HOURS AND FIREFIGHTING.** Workloads are not evenly distributed across a project's lifecycle. Some phases require intensive effort from specific resources, while others leave them idle. This imbalance leads to inefficiencies, with teams experiencing periods of underutilization followed by high-pressure sprints to recover lost time.

● **PROJECT MANAGERS HOARD RESOURCES.** Resource assignment is a frequent source of tension. Project managers fiercely guard their allocated resources, ensuring they have what they need to meet deadlines and avoid delays. Meanwhile, higher management seeks to optimize efficiency by reallocating resources across projects, often disrupting plans and creating conflicts over availability and priorities.

THE VISCOUS CYCLE

Review the vicious cycle with your team to ensure alignment on the core challenge:

The need for resources fluctuates during the project life cycle—there are peaks and valleys in the need for resources (#1). Since there are not enough skilled resources that can be dedicated to each project (#2) in some cases, resources are not available when needed (#3). In turn the shortage in needed resources creates work stoppages and when work is done by less than optimal resources it takes even longer and involves rework (#4). Consequently,

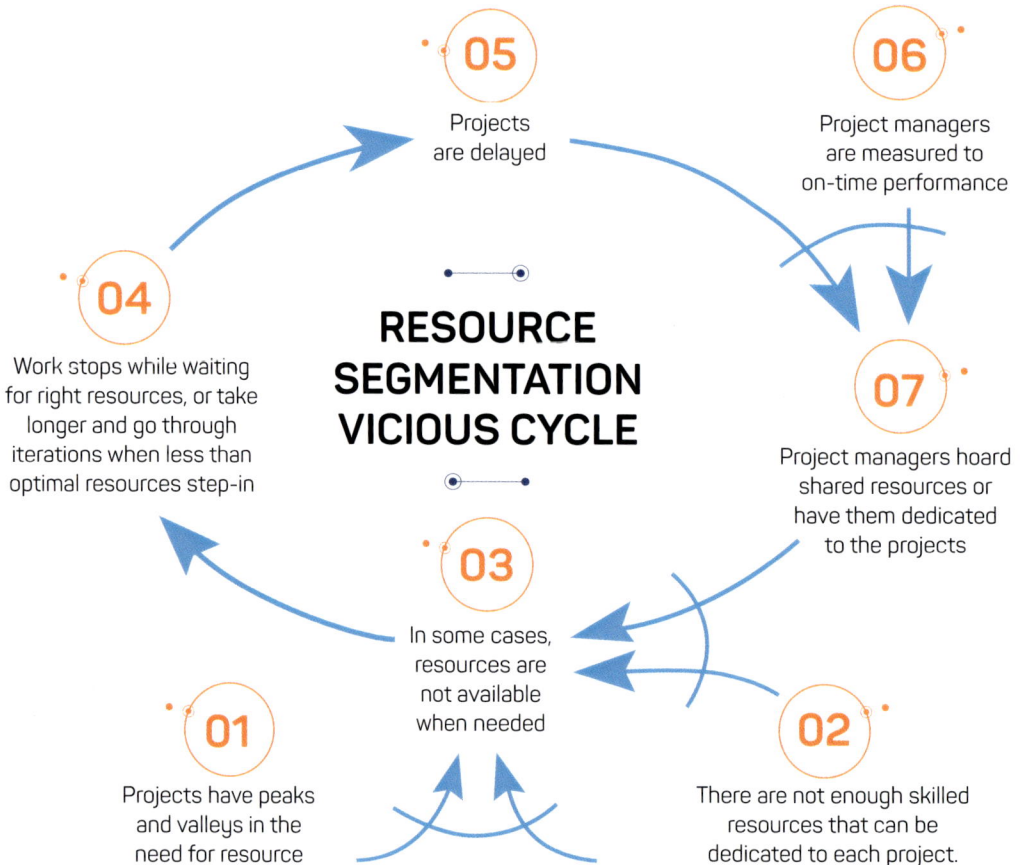

05 Projects are delayed

06 Project managers are measured to on-time performance

04 Work stops while waiting for right resources, or take longer and go through iterations when less than optimal resources step-in

RESOURCE SEGMENTATION VICIOUS CYCLE

07 Project managers hoard shared resources or have them dedicated to the projects

03 In some cases, resources are not available when needed

01 Projects have peaks and valleys in the need for resource

02 There are not enough skilled resources that can be dedicated to each project.

projects are delayed (#5). Since project managers are measured to on-time performance (#6) they hoard shared resources and place pressure to dedicate them to their projects (#7). Once segmented to their projects it is very difficult to utilize these resources to other assignments. Resources are then rendered not available when needed (#3).

THE SOLUTION

The key to breaking this vicious cycle is to share resources across projects while ensuring each project receives the needed resources in a timely manner. When resources are dedicated to specific projects, staffing must be based on these projects' peak demand. However, resource shortages often occur because there aren't enough resources to meet all peak demands simultaneously across all projects.

By pooling resources instead of dedicating them to individual projects, these peaks can be balanced. The peak demand of one project rarely aligns perfectly with another, allowing the shared resource pool to support more projects with the same overall capacity. This approach reduces bottlenecks, improves efficiency, and ensures better utilization of available resources.

The following figure illustrates the fluctuating demand for the same type of resources in two projects (Project A and Project B) over time. For example, on week 1, Project A requires 7 resources, while Project B requires 4. Each project has been allocated 6 resources, as represented by the dotted line. However, this fixed allocation leads to shortages at peak demand points. In Project A, there aren't enough resources on weeks 1, 5 and 7, while in Project B, demand exceeds capacity on weeks 3, 6, and 9. These shortages cause delays in both projects. To fully meet demand without delays, we would need 8 resources for Project A and 9 for Project B - a total of 17 resources. The right-side figure shows the combined demand across both projects over time. Notably, the peaks and valleys offset each other. For example, on week 3, Project B needs 9 resources, while Project A only requires 3. Across the entire timeline, the peak combined demand is 12 resources (on weeks 3, 6, and 7).

It means that by pooling resources instead of allocating them separately, we can ensure that the 12 available resources are used efficiently to meet demand across both projects. This approach eliminates shortages, prevents delays, and maximizes resource utilization without increasing overall staffing.

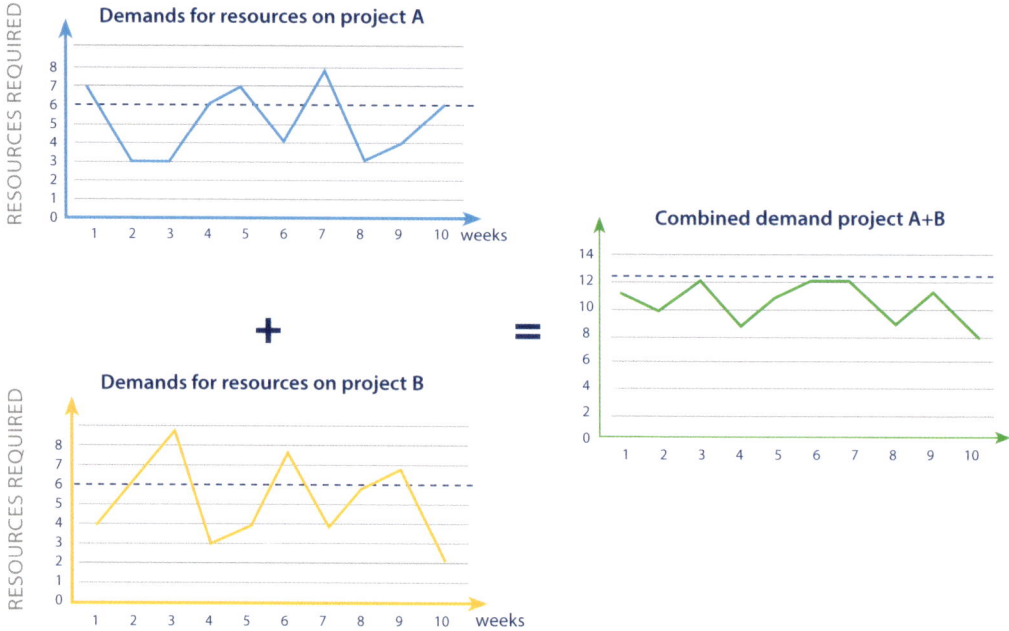

Resource Pooling

Pooling resources across multiple projects must be done with careful consideration, ensuring that it doesn't jeopardize the projects to which they were originally assigned. The transition should ultimately build stakeholders' confidence that a shared resource pool will enhance resource availability for every project - far more than the current state, where each project periodically suffers from shortages during peaks in demand. The process to move from dedicated resources to a common pool that serves multiple projects is therefore as follows:

STEP 1 | DECIDE WHICH RESOURCES SHOULD REMAIN DEDICATED AND WHICH SHOULD BE POOLED. In some cases, resources develop contextual knowledge about a project that takes time to acquire. This knowledge is particularly crucial when integrating work across different disciplines, as misalignment can lead to delays and inefficiencies. To mitigate this risk, some resources must remain dedicated to the project to maintain continuity and ensure integration runs smoothly. For example, in an engineering project developing a complex system requiring mechanical, electrical, and software expertise, a core group of engineers from each discipline should remain dedicated. These dedicated resources handle the non-standard work that relies on deep project knowledge, while pooled resources can take on more standardized tasks. When assigning work to the pooled resources it is important to ensure that the work is indeed standardized. Often, pooling needs to be accompanied by a robust Full-kit process to ensure that the pooled resources do not get stuck when performing their tasks (see Chapter 7 on Standardization: transitioning experts from doing the work to guiding less experienced people in effectively performing non-standard tasks). In other kinds of projects, it is possible to pool all the resources. For instance, in projects like construction the resources can be more completely pooled since the work is generally more standardized.

STEP 2 | IMPLEMENT A LOW WIP PROJECT PIPELINING PROCESS BEFORE YOU POOL RESOURCES! Reducing the WIP of projects minimizes multitasking and improves the productivity of the resources. Once resources are more focused the flow of project work will be smoother decreasing peaks and valleys. Moreover, by staggering projects in the pipeline we can ensure that the total resources needed across all the projects is less than the total resources available in the combined pool. When project managers see how reduced WIP makes resources available - and when they observe that the pooled resource capacity is sufficient - they will become more comfortable with the system and be more willing to release resources. For a more detailed explanation of the pipelining process, see Chapter 8 on Synchronization: creating a work plan using the drum mechanism.

STEP 3 | IMPLEMENT A SINGLE PRIORITY LIST ACROSS PROJECTS. Develop a method for prioritizing tasks across projects. In some cases, prioritization can be based on project due dates, giving higher priority to tasks in projects with earlier deadlines. However, to prioritize projects at higher risk of being late a more sophisticated approach is often needed. This mechanism is detailed in Chapter 9 on Time Buffers: Establishing a Buffer Management Mechanism for Fast Response. Projects where the critical chain progresses more slowly than buffer consumption are marked Red on the fever chart and are given higher priority. As a result, shared resources will be allocated to tasks on these projects first.

STEP 4 | IMPLEMENT ORGANIZATIONAL CHANGES ONLY WHEN THE BENEFITS OF POOLING ARE ESTABLISHED. In some cases, the resources are dedicated to the project based on an organizational structure. For example, in the case of the Air Force base, the resources are part of different squadrons. In this situation, it is often necessary to change the organizational structure to create a sustainable pooling solution that can deliver on the full benefits. However, organizational changes often come with unintended consequences - new reporting lines, performance metrics, and unfamiliar colleagues - which can be unsettling. To minimize disruption, pooling should be implemented gradually. The first step is establishing a common task priority list to allocate resources across projects from different organizations. This is typically managed in a joint meeting where project representatives use the priority list to assign resources effectively. Only after the benefits of pooling are demonstrated should structural changes be considered. Organizational restructuring should be the final step, ensuring a smooth transition to a fully integrated resource pool.

Technicians at an Air Force base. To solve the problem of skilled maintenance technicians the first step was to implement a low WIP solution for aircraft maintenance in both squadrons. The low WIP implementation reduced the number of jobs that were active and needed support. Next, maintenance tasks from both squadrons were combined into a single priority list, and a daily management meeting was introduced to allocate resources effectively. Jobs were prioritized to maximize aircraft availability across both squadrons. Supervisors jointly managed the list, dynamically moving resources to ensure effective resource utilization and minimize delays in aircraft maintenance.

While this approach successfully streamlined workload management, technicians raised concerns about skills development and career progression under the new system. To address these concerns, organizational integration became necessary. Once the resource assignment process was well-established and the benefits of pooling were validated through both experience and data, the transition to a unified management structure was initiated. This change was supported by extensive communication and proactive engagement to address concerns. A new organizational identity was established, reinforcing a shared mission to achieve higher aircraft availability. With strong leadership and effective change management, the restructuring successfully cemented the pooling process, ensuring a sustainable solution and workforce engagement.

Software developers in a telecom IT provider. To introduce resource pooling, the organization adopted a matrix structure where software developers were organized into "lines" and allocated to projects based on budget forecasts. This shift was necessitated by the transition from time-and-material contracts to fixed-price contracts, which intensified budget constraints.

Under this system, projects were assigned dedicated resources for their entire duration or specific phases, depending on budget allocations. However, line managers, under pressure to maintain profitability, had little flexibility to retain extra resources. Most developers were fully deployed, leaving only a few between assignments.

This rigid allocation led to significant challenges when project scope changes or rework cycles required more resources than initially planned. As a result, projects frequently faced skill-specific resource shortages, causing delays, fire-fighting, and excessive workloads for developers.

To address these issues, the organization implemented Critical Chain Project Management (CCPM) (see Chapters 8 on Synchronization: create a plan of work using the drum mechanism and Chapter 9 on Time Buffers: aggregating buffers). Instead of assigning full-budgeted resources to projects, CCPM challenged built-in safety margins and transitioned to plans with explicit time and budget buffers. These budget buffers were then pooled at the line level, enabling the creation of a centrally managed resource pool.

Funded by project budgets but managed centrally, this shared resource pool provided surge capacity across all projects, helping to absorb fluctuations in demand. By combining CCPM with resource pooling, the organization improved due-date performance while reducing the strain on developers, ensuring more effective project execution.

Experts in a startup. As the medical device manufacturer expanded rapidly, effectively utilizing expert resources became critical (for a refresher on this issue, see Chapter 7 on Standardization: The Challenge, Indicators, and Vicious Cycle). With multiple new product development projects leveraging the same core technology, the company faced increasing complexity. Each project targeted different disease endpoints and markets while needing to meet stringent regulatory requirements.

Initially, the experts who developed the technology were assigned as managers for different projects. However, because their specialized knowledge was frequently needed across multiple projects, waiting for their availability caused delays, hindered the development of newer team members, and triggered rework cycles that threatened project quality and timelines.

To address this bottleneck, the company took a radical step - pooling expert resources and transitioning them out of management roles. These experts were reassigned as technical authorities rather than project managers, allowing them to support multiple projects instead of being tied to a single one. Management roles were backfilled with capable managers, ensuring operational continuity while freeing experts to focus on high-value technical work.

The experts were given technical authority to Full-kit project phases and tasks. This meant that they prepared project work upfront, ensuring that when tasks were launched, all necessary elements were in place to avoid delays and rework. To support this shift, projects were structured into clearly defined Full-kit phases, and execution was pipelined based on the availability of expert resources to prepare the work (see Chapter 8 on Synchronization: creating a work plan using the drum mechanism).

While this transition required pausing some projects and tasks until they were Full-kit, the impact was transformational:

● Work across all projects accelerated,

● New resources were trained more effectively, and

● The quality of products and regulatory compliance improved without compromise.

Engineers in an aerospace OEM. In an aerospace OEM, engineers were measured based on how long they remained on overhead, creating pressure to keep them on projects longer than necessary and leading resource managers to push engineers onto projects prematurely. This resulted in resource shortages in some projects, underutilization in others, and engineers starting work without all necessary inputs, causing rework cycles and quality issues. To address this, the company first improved work execution by implementing WIP boards across teams to establish Full-Kit and enable focused execution. The project plans were built with milestones where resources would be added to the project. While the company already followed a gated process, time pressures often led teams to bypass gate criteria, moving forward before completing prior phases. To prevent this, a buffer-based plan was introduced, allowing teams to wait for proper completion before progressing. Resource movement between projects was then better managed by assigning engineers only when work was fully kitted, ensuring they could be immediately effective. This change required revisiting acceptable overhead levels, adjusting project planning and execution, and ensuring projects were properly staged.

HOW TO CAUSE THE CHANGE

Transitioning from segmented resources to pooled resources must be handled carefully, as various stakeholders have genuine concerns. The key challenges and solutions include:

● MANAGING ORGANIZATIONAL CHANGE AND IDENTITY CONCERNS

Organizational changes often come with unintended consequences. People associate their identity with their current team, and restructuring can be unsettling - introducing a new boss, new performance metrics, and unfamiliar colleagues. Resources may also worry about their career paths and feel disconnected from projects they once identified with, potentially losing motivation and commitment. To mitigate this, pooling should initially be implemented without formal organizational changes. Once the benefits of pooling are evident, structural changes can be introduced with a strong emphasis on fostering a culture of technical excellence as a substitute for the pride of belonging to a specific project.

● MAINTAINING PROJECT CONTRIBUTION AND FOCUS

Dedicated resources contribute to projects beyond their specific skills, often demonstrating higher commitment to project goals. Pooling may dilute this sense of ownership, leading to concerns about project performance. To address this, not all resources should be pooled - some should remain dedicated to ensure project continuity. Collaborating with project teams to define the optimal level of pooling can help protect project interests while pooling sufficient resources to gain the benefits.

● ALLEVIATING PROJECT MANAGERS' FEARS OF LOSING CONTROL

Project managers accustomed to "owning" their resources may struggle with the idea of relying on a shared pool. They fear that resources will not be available when needed, jeopardizing project commitments. This perception of losing control can be countered by implementing a low-WIP project pipeline. When project managers see how reduced WIP improves speed and productivity - and when they observe that the pooled resource capacity is sufficient - they will become more comfortable with the system and be more willing to release resources.

● ENSURING RESOURCE MANAGERS CAN ASSIGN THE RIGHT RESOURCES TO THE RIGHT TASKS

Pooled resource managers face the challenge of prioritizing work across multiple projects. Without a clear allocation method, they may find themselves forced to make tough decisions, potentially being perceived as unfair or biased. To prevent this, a priority criteria should be established and agreed upon by all project managers. This ensures that the resource manager's role is well-defined, preventing arbitrary decisions and ensuring resources are allocated effectively to maximize project success.

● FUNDING THE COMMON POOL OF RESOURCES

When resources are not assigned to a project, they are typically considered overhead. In many organizations, overhead is viewed as waste. When resources are pooled, there is a concern that at times, some resources will not be assigned to project tasks, leading to an increase in overhead. To enable resource pooling, the organization must establish a funding mechanism for these resources. One approach is to increase the overhead budget with top management's agreement, ensuring it does not raise the overall resource budget. Another option is to allocate a portion of each project's budget to fund the pool, with project managers understanding that this will ultimately increase resource availability. It's important to note that pooling resources actually improves productivity, allowing more projects to be completed with the same resources. The challenge is establishing a common funding mechanism to enable this productivity gain.

By gradually implementing pooling, addressing stakeholder concerns proactively, and reinforcing the benefits of low-WIP execution, the transition to a pooled resource model can be successful while maintaining organizational stability, project performance, and workforce motivation.

GUIDING QUESTIONS FOR GROUP DISCUSSION & IMPLEMENTATION

Follow these guiding questions to facilitate a discussion with your team on resource pooling:

IDENTIFY RESOURCES THAT SHOULD BE POOLED

1   Which resources are short across many projects?

2   Which resources are firefighting and spending the most "overtime"?

3   Are these resources dedicated to projects?

DECIDE WHICH RESOURCES TO POOL AND WHICH SHOULD REMAIN DEDICATED

4   Does the project involve integration of work of multiple disciplines?
    Will this integration require dedicated resources on the project?

5   Do the resources need to have contextual knowledge of the project (such as relationship with the customer, the history of the project etc.)?

6   Is there standard work that can be performed by less experienced (pooled) resources?

7   Are there experts who are needed across projects to Full-kit the work?

DECIDE ON THE GATES AND MILESTONES WHERE RESOURCES WILL BE ADDED TO OR LEAVE THE PROJECT

8   Are the resources needed for a phase of the project?

9   Can the project be organized into stages with gates? Can the gates be synchronized with the addition of resources to the project?

10 Are there adequate buffers in the project to allow the project to be held while the stage is being Full-kitted?

DECIDE HOW TO MANAGE THE POOLED RESOURCES

11 Is there a way to prioritize tasks across projects?

12 Is there a need to implement CCPM and buffer management to obtain task priorities?

13 Do the projects have budget buffers to fund resources "on the bench"?

14 How will the resources performance be evaluated?

15 How will the resources be motivated to contribute across all projects?

11
CHAPTER

IMPROVING PROJECT FLOW

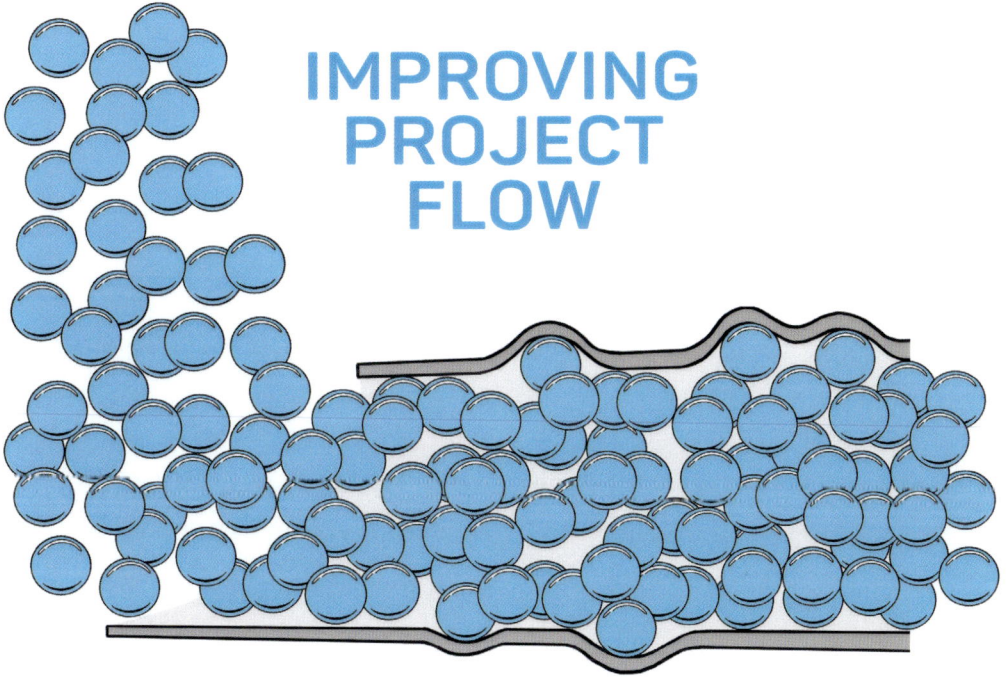

FOCUS STARTS WITH WHAT TO STOP DOING

To get the full picture, it's important to take a step back and understand how come despite massive efforts to address the challenges in project-based environments, organizations keep facing them again and again. We need to realize which common practices are leading us in the wrong direction and make a conscious decision to avoid these pitfalls. As Dr. Eliyahu Goldratt often said: "Focus starts with what to stop doing."

In our efforts to bring order, we often establish processes and measurements aimed at maximizing the productivity of every resource and department. We assign project managers to ensure the objectives of each project are met. However, these efforts frequently result in greatly overloading the system with open work. Everyone focuses on starting projects and tasks as early as possible, open more jobs and creating pressure to push work forward even when it's not ready. When the system is flooded with open work, we lose the ability to focus and complete tasks effectively. Multitasking becomes rampant, with constant switching between tasks. Resources are spread too thin, leaving insufficient capacity to complete work properly. Tasks are started without adequate preparation, leading to frequent stoppages and rework. This overload and its consequences make it much harder to synchronize resources and activities.

In our pursuit of predictability, we often create highly detailed project plans, meticulously scheduling activities and resources. While these plans may give an illusion of clarity, the reality is that as work progresses uncertainties emerge, and the gap between the plan and actual events grows rapidly. Team members stop relying on the plans, and the chaos we sought to control resurfaces, stronger than ever. This cycle not only undermines our goals of agility, reliability, and productivity but also reinforces the very chaos we're trying to eliminate.

When challenges escalate and things start to spiral out of control, managers often turn to a set of common tactics. Unfortunately, these tactics rarely address the root causes of the problems and, in some cases, even make them worse. We call these *The Seductive Seven*[6] approaches that give the illusion of progress but fail to deliver real and sustainable

---

[6] For more information on The Seductive Seven: Ashlag, Y. & Cox, K. (2020). *Stop Decorating the Fish*. North River Press Publishing Corporation.

solutions. As you explore The Seductive Seven, think about times when these tactics were used in your organization. Did they truly improve outcomes, or were they merely surface-level fixes that left the fundamental issues unchanged? Reflect on whether they led to any substantial, lasting improvements.

SEDUCTIVE TACTIC | 1 | MORE RESOURCES

When struggling to complete more projects faster, a common response is to demand more resources. On the surface, this seems logical - after all, isn't the problem a lack of capacity? One critical flaw in this approach is the assumption that current operations are already optimized. Instead of examining and improving how we use the resources we have, we stick to the same practices and simply demand more. It means that we leave the inefficiencies in place. Moreover, if adding resources were the simple solution, why hasn't it already been done? The reality is additional resources often come with challenges. Skilled resources are hard to find and expensive. Consequently, organizations often hire less experienced people, which creates more work for overwhelmed experts who now have to train newcomers and correct their mistakes. This increases delays and rework, as progress stalls while waiting for expert input. Additionally, when budgets are approved to bring in more resources, they are often tied to expectations of taking on even more work. As a result, the same underlying issues persist, just on a larger scale. In summary, this approach fails to address the challenges and perpetuates the cycle of overburden and delays.

SEDUCTIVE TACTIC | 2 | MORE DATA

We often believe that more data will lead to greater visibility and predictability. This mindset frequently results in overly detailed plans filled with thousands of tasks that attempt to anticipate every contingency and risk. While this approach may seem logical, in practice, it often backfires. Overly detailed plans quickly become a liability. Conditions are constantly changing, making it nearly impossible to keep the plans updated. The more intricate the plans, the harder it is to align them with reality. In many cases, there is an army of people just to keep these plans updated and yet the plans still fall behind and do not reflect reality. Eventually the plans get abandoned as a tool for managing project execution. True predictability is not achieved by imposing certainty (detailed plans) on uncertainty (reality). Instead, predictability comes from addressing the key sources of disruption in our own practices. By reducing these self-inflicted disruptions, we can develop plans that are simple, adaptable, and provide sufficient predictability despite the unavoidable uncertainties that remain.

SEDUCTIVE TACTIC | 3 | MORE ACCOUNTABILITY

In project environments, there is often a strong focus on measurements and compliance to create order and ensure progress towards meeting deadlines. While this emphasis may seem reasonable, these measures are frequently implemented without addressing the broken processes that cause delays and budget overruns in the first place. As a result, when projects fall behind, such metrics create counterproductive behaviors. Team members may focus on completing easier tasks while avoiding riskier or more complex ones, increasing the chances of delays later in the project. Additionally, the pressure to meet deadlines often leads team members to include extra safety buffers in their task estimates. As experienced managers know, once these buffers are built into the schedule, they tend to be used up - even when they aren't truly necessary. Simply adding measurements and compliance mechanisms without fixing the underlying issues often leads to frustration and makes the problems worse. To achieve meaningful progress, it's essential to address the root causes rather than relying solely on accountability measures.

SEDUCTIVE TACTIC | 4 | MORE TECHNOLOGY

Faced with the high variability in task durations and the difficulty of synchronizing resources and activities, many organizations turn to technology. Significant resources are invested in implementing project management technology tools, with the hope that they will streamline processes and improve outcomes. However, these tools rarely address the underlying practices that cause projects to miss deadlines. Instead, they often reinforce existing inefficiencies by embedding flawed practices into their design. For example, they may encourage early start of activities resulting in higher WIP; they may motivate creating cumbersome project plans with thousands of activities; and they may embed tasks level metrics that drive wrong behaviors like inserting buffers into task durations etc. As a result, rather than solving the core problems, these tools institutionalize mistakes and make them harder to fix. Technology can be a powerful enabler, but it must reinforce the right behaviors, otherwise, it becomes just another source of inertia in the organization.

SEDUCTIVE TACTIC | 5 | MORE STRATEGIC PLANNING

When projects fail to meet their objectives, the instinctive response is often to revise the strategy and launch new initiatives. This typically results in adding even more projects to an already overwhelmed system. In many cases, projects are even halted midway to make room for these new priorities. However, if the root problem isn't in the strategy but in the execution - in how we manage the workflow - this approach only exacerbates the situation. Adding more initiatives without fixing the execution issues spreads resources even thinner, increases inefficiencies, and further delays progress. Re-strategizing is important, but if execution flaws remain unaddressed, it risks becoming yet another source of chaos.

SEDUCTIVE TACTIC | 6 | MORE TRAINING

Often, organizations attempt to improve their operations by training individuals in doing their work more efficiently. While training may improve the actual time it takes to perform the tasks, it typically does not address waiting times and rework. It is more of a local solution that does not address the friction in the way work flows through the organization. Moreover, when we authorize a certain training, we assume that it will bring about a desirable behavioral change. However, if we do not make it easy and natural for people to take the desired actions, and specifically, if the measures, the processes, the way the system runs conflict with the behaviors we want to encourage, then training alone would be insufficient. We first need to design the work environment, so it is natural for people to behave in line with the training they undergo. This calls for a more systematic approach to dealing with core practices affecting the flow of work through the organization.

SEDUCTIVE TACTIC | 7 | MORE REORGANIZATION

Reorganizing is often seen as a way to address underperformance and achieve goals. For example, we may centralize operations to improve efficiency and reduce finger-pointing between teams. However, it's usually just a matter of time before we shift back—formally or informally—to decentralization, aiming to enhance accountability and speed up work completion by local teams. The fact that organizations frequently toggle between these structures highlights a key issue: reorganization alone is not a sufficient solution. It often fails to address the underlying problems that disrupt the workflow and merely shifts the accountability for these problems. Worse still, if executed poorly, reorganization can create additional chaos and further disrupt the flow of work. True improvement requires addressing the root causes of inefficiencies first, and then determining which structural changes can support and enhance the new processes.

The seven tactics discussed can play a supportive role in strengthening and scaling solutions aimed at enhancing performance, but they are not sufficient on their own. To achieve meaningful progress, it is essential to focus on improving flow of project work. By identifying the major obstacles to flow that cause disruptions and implementing effective solutions to streamline operations, we can then leverage resources, technology, training, metrics, data, and organizational structure to reinforce and sustain these improvements.

FOCUS ON FLOW

Eli Goldratt said that "Improving Flow (or equivalently lead time) is a primary objective of operations". It is important to remind ourselves why it is primary. The immediate benefits of improving flow are directly tied to improving productivity – doing more projects with the same resources and completing them faster. These benefits are accompanied by improvements to the quality of the deliverables as well. When work flows smoothly, people are focused and make fewer mistakes, they tend to care more about the outcomes and can often go the extra mile to deliver extraordinary results. These benefits in productivity, speed and quality can often be leveraged into a competitive advantage for the organization. New products that make a bigger impact on the market, IT projects that deliver real value to the organization, capital projects that finish on time and meet or exceed their business goals, maintenance and repair projects that deliver faster and extend the time between failures, service projects that deliver on customized value to the customer. In almost every case delivering on one project faster is important but having the capability to deliver on a pipeline of projects with speed, productivity and higher quality can be a game changing advantage.

Improving flow is not only a competitive advantage but also one that is difficult to match. When we focus on flow as the primary objective, we are forced to re-examine the rooted disruptive practices and policies embedded in the way we manage projects. Changing these practices requires leadership commitment to implement changes that often seem to go against conventional wisdom. It requires perseverance, continuous effort and subordination of the entire organization to the principles of Theory of Constraints. This is not easy! But this difficulty is what makes it a competitive advantage that you can defend for long periods of time. The organization that takes the lead in adopting this primacy of flow continues to build on this lead over its competitors.

This implementation guidebook can help to structure this journey and the underlying thinking. It can help you identify the Obstacles to Flow that need to be tackled. It can help you come up with a physical change that you can implement. It can help you generate the early success stories that can fuel the cultural change necessary for long term success. So get ready, set - plan your actions according to the recommended steps in chapter 1, and go.

TOC SOLUTION	FLOW OBSTACLE
TRIAGE THE PROJECTS Triage the projects to select and scope the few projects that make a significant impact on the goal.	When a surfeit of low-value projects disrupts the focus on and progress of high-value projects, delaying their completion and compromising the scope and quality of their outcomes.
REDUCE BAD MULTITASKING Control the WIP of projects and tasks at the organization/department/resource level.	When team members switch among too many projects and tasks without completing any.
SEGREGATE BIG & SMALL TASKS Segregate by time or resources low-load and high-load tasks.	When the same team members handle a mix of low-load and high-load jobs, ending up compromising the delivery of all jobs.
ENSURE FULL-KIT Devote management attention to full-kitting projects and project phases and implement a strict Full-kit discipline.	When too often, projects, or project phases, come to a halt or require rework because they were initiated without all the necessary requirements to adequately complete the job.

TOC SOLUTION	FLOW OBSTACLE
INCREASE WORK DOSAGE Increase task work dosage to complete them faster or extend the time until they return for further work.	When the pressure to address many tasks leads to reducing the scope of work when performing each task, causing them to frequently return for further work.
STANDARDIZE TO SCALE Effectively utilize experts' capacity to scale and standardize the work. Move experts from doing the work to full-kitting the work.	When too often work carried out by less experienced workers \ falls short, necessitates rework, and poses challenges to scaling without compromising work quality.
SYNCHRONIZE RESOURCES & ACTIVITIES Establish a Drum mechanism to restrict the WIP of activities and sequence them according to a single global priority scheme.	When team members prioritize tasks based on local considerations, which are often not aligned with global priorities, thereby causing delays that are typically discovered in later stages of the project.
AGGREGATE & MANAGE TIME BUFFERS Aggregate buffers from the task level to the project level to protect the Critical Chain. Measure progress on the Critical Chain against buffer consumption to assess project status and identify the need for recovery actions.	When the common perception that there aren't enough buffers leads team members to add whatever buffers they can to each task in the project. This approach wastes the very buffers needed to handle critical disruptions and uncertainty.
POOL RESOURCES Create a common pool of resources to address the peaks in demand across all projects, ensuring projects receive adequate resources when required.	When resources are segmented to specific projects, shortages arise where demand is high, while surpluses build up where they are underutilized. This rigidity reduces flexibility and slows overall project flow.